Mobility & Politics

Series editors
Martin Geiger
Carleton University
Ottawa, Canada

Parvati Raghuram
Open University
Milton Keynes, UK

William Walters
Carleton University
Ottawa, Canada

Mobility & Politics

Series Editors: Martin Geiger, Carleton University, Ottawa, Canada; Parvati Raghuram, Open University, Milton Keynes, UK; William Walters, Carleton University, Ottawa, Canada

Global Advisory Board: Michael Collyer, University of Sussex; Susan B. Coutin, University of California; Raúl Delgado Wise, Universidad Autónoma de Zacatecas; Nicholas De Genova, King's College London; Eleonore Kofman, Middlesex University; Rey Koslowski, University at Albany; Loren B. Landau, University of the Witwatersrand; Sandro Mezzadra, Università di Bologna; Alison Mountz, Wilfrid Laurier University; Brett Neilson, University of Western Sydney; Antoine Pécoud, Université Paris 13; Ranabir Samaddar, Mahanirban Research Group Calcutta; Nandita Sharma, University of Hawai'i at Manoa; Tesfaye Tafesse, Addis Ababa University; Thanh-Dam Truong, Erasmus University Rotterdam.

Human mobility, whatever its scale, is often controversial. Hence it carries with it the potential for politics. A core feature of mobility politics is the tension between the desire to maximise the social and economic benefits of migration and pressures to restrict movement. Transnational communities, global instability, advances in transportation and communication, and concepts of 'smart borders' and 'migration management' are just a few of the phenomena transforming the landscape of migration today. The tension between openness and restriction raises important questions about how different types of policy and politics come to life and influence mobility.

Mobility & Politics invites original, theoretically and empirically informed studies for academic and policy-oriented debates. Authors examine issues such as refugees and displacement, migration and citizenship, security and cross-border movements, (post-)colonialism and mobility, and transnational movements and cosmopolitics.

More information about this series at
http://www.palgrave.com/gp/series/14800

Alex Sager

Toward a Cosmopolitan Ethics of Mobility

The Migrant's-Eye View of the World

Alex Sager
Philosophy
Portland State University
Portland, OR, USA

Mobility & Politics
ISBN 978-3-319-88098-3   ISBN 978-3-319-65759-2 (eBook)
https://doi.org/10.1007/978-3-319-65759-2

Library of Congress Control Number: 2017957618

© The Editor(s) (if applicable) and The Author(s) 2018
Softcover reprint of the hardcover 1st edition 2018   978-3-319-65758-5
This work is subject to copyright. All rights are solely and exclusively licensed by the Publisher, whether the whole or part of the material is concerned, specifically the rights of translation, reprinting, reuse of illustrations, recitation, broadcasting, reproduction on microfilms or in any other physical way, and transmission or information storage and retrieval, electronic adaptation, computer software, or by similar or dissimilar methodology now known or hereafter developed.
The use of general descriptive names, registered names, trademarks, service marks, etc. in this publication does not imply, even in the absence of a specific statement, that such names are exempt from the relevant protective laws and regulations and therefore free for general use.
The publisher, the authors and the editors are safe to assume that the advice and information in this book are believed to be true and accurate at the date of publication. Neither the publisher nor the authors or the editors give a warranty, express or implied, with respect to the material contained herein or for any errors or omissions that may have been made. The publisher remains neutral with regard to jurisdictional claims in published maps and institutional affiliations.

Cover illustration: Modern building window © saulgranda/Getty

Printed on acid-free paper

This Palgrave Macmillan imprint is published by Springer Nature
The registered company is Springer International Publishing AG
The registered company address is: Gewerbestrasse 11, 6330 Cham, Switzerland

Series Editors' Foreword

People are on the move, but then again, haven't we always been? What's new is not migration, but the many technologies coalescing around the modern state to allow the 'correct' people to move while denying mobility to others. National technologies like passports or multi-scalar boundaries operate more like membranes rather than walls, making value judgements on people with its de-facto state's-eye view.

In this important contribution to the philosophy of migration, *Alex Sager* makes a convincing case to embrace the migrant's-eye view and, in doing so, break free from the methodological nationalism that contours and limits social science research in migration studies and normative philosophy.

For scholars of all stripes—geographers to philosophers, political scientists and sociologists alike—*Toward a Cosmopolitan Ethics of Mobility* is both a timely as well as important intervention because it carves out an explicit space within which to imagine an ethic of migration that needs not to be anchored to the perceived inevitability of the nation state. The state, one of many creatures of modernity, has played a structuring role in how we come to think about human migration. In an age of accelerating migration due to modern excesses, including (but not limited to) disaster capitalism, war or man-made environmental insecurity, it is increasingly important to free ourselves from the intellectual limit of bordered thinking to confront the pressing social issues ahead.

Alex Sager makes a case for an ethic of migration that is cognizant of the ways in which methodological nationalism places the ethical burden on those who move rather than on the institution that seeks to prevent movement. In questioning the state's right to 'illegalize' people, we see how the embodied migrant's humanity is attended to rather than the largely imagined body of the state. Nuancing an ethic of migration in this way, the work escapes the dualism of thick borders or no borders by instead asking readers to shift the burden of ethical proof away from an assumed bad migrant. Building from developments in border studies, the author reminds us that bordering happens at various points of migration. Importantly, his contribution makes a case for putting into practice an ethical framework that sees international refugee movements and municipal gentrification as part of a spectrum rather than as discrete problems.

Toward a Cosmopolitan Ethics of Mobility makes an important contribution to our ongoing series-length conversation about mobility politics and the multiple connections between mobility and politics. By connecting social issues such as gentrification (largely seen as a municipal level concern), internal displacements (largely seen as a national concern) and transnational migration (largely seen as an international concern), the challenge posed in the book is to look at the structure that connects these multi-scalar issues rather than continuing to treat them in isolation. This opens meaningful and necessary conceptual and normative space to deepen our conversations.

The Series Editors:
Martin Geiger, Carleton University
Parvati Raghuram, Open University
William Walters, Carleton University

and

Ajay Parasram, Dalhousie University and
Mobility & Politics Research Collective
www.mobpoli.info / www.mobilitypoliticsseries.com

PREFACE

A little over two decades ago, I migrated from small town in northern Canada to the modest metropolis of Calgary and stumbled into a philosophy class. What attracted me to philosophy (a discipline alien to the public school system) was the process of grappling with difficult, often baffling, ideas and texts, followed by the moments of insight which broadened and transformed my view of the world. Philosophy unsettles our assumptions and, if we are fortunate, leads to the exhilaration of seeing the world a new. This brief monograph explores two insights about migration that have begun to change how I see the world.

The first insight—in hindsight of embarrassing simplicity—was that migration is an ethical issue. The violence of migration restrictions is largely invisible to people whose citizenship provides them with extensive free movement. As with many people working in analytic political philosophy, Joseph Carens' work was a revelation.[1] As Carens made clear, it is hard to reconcile restrictive and coercive immigration policies with respect for many fundamental rights and freedoms of movement, opportunity, and association that we take for granted inside nation-states. From Carens I went back to Michael Walzer's profound (though I think in many respects mistaken) chapter on membership in *Spheres of Justice* (1983) and moved forward to Phillip Cole's *Philosophies of Exclusion* (2000).

The second insight was that the cognitive bias of methodological nationalism shapes how we see and act in the world. The nation-state has sought to remake the world in its own image. In this it has failed, but to a large extent it has successfully shaped how we see the world—for example, statistics are almost invariably provided by nation-states and collected within their boundaries. Methodological nationalism not only shapes policy, but also the social sciences. For me, a catalyst was Andreas Wimmer and Nina Glick Schiller's "Methodological Nationalism and Beyond: Nation-State Building, Migration and the Social Sciences" (2002). By the time the article crossed my path, many fields had acknowledged the role of nation-building in producing knowledge about their disciplines. Nonetheless, it was new to me and (I venture) to most political philosophers who have yet to assimilate methodological nationalism's relevance to normative theory.

This is not surprising. Political philosophy and political theory are notoriously slow in assimilating empirical literature. Rainer Bauböck observes:

> The weakness of political theory is that it takes a long time to digest insights of other disciplines about changing structures of modern societies, including those changes that we associate with transnationalism. Its strength lies in the striving for analytical consistence in conceptual analysis and normative judgments. (Bauböck 2010: 296)[2]

Despite efforts to "talk across disciplines" in migration studies, much research remains in disciplinary silos.[3] Though some philosophers have closely engaged with economics, political philosophy largely remains estranged from exciting work on migration by anthropologists, geographers, historians, and sociologists who are challenging us to rethink at a fundamental level how we should conceive of mobility and territory. This is unfortunate for the philosophers and for social scientists who would also gain from more closely engaging political philosophy.

Toward a Cosmopolitan Ethics of Mobility[4] is a modest attempt to digest some of the insights from other disciplines in the quest for analytic consistency for our normative judgments. It is a metaphilosophical endeavor, more than a substantive one. I do not try to lay out a normative theory of mobility or of borders; instead, I attempt to draw attention to considerations that should ground such a theory. My hope is that this will serve my own efforts in thinking about these questions and inspire dialogue among colleagues across disciplines.

Portland, OR, USA   Alex Sager

Notes

1. Carens' "Migration and Morality: A Liberal Egalitarian Perspective" (1992) was my introduction to the topic. For many other philosophers it was his "Aliens and Citizens: The Case for Open Borders" (1987).
2. I use "political theory" and "political philosophy" interchangeably in this monograph. As far as I have been able to determine, these labels—at least in the United States—mostly reflect whether one's degree and employment is in a political science department or a philosophy department. Though various people have suggested more deep-set differences, there is no agreed-upon distinction between the two terms.
3. A shortcoming of Caroline Brettel and James Hollifield's excellent *Migration Theory: Talking Across Disciplines* (2008) is that limited "talking across disciplines" takes place: most of the chapters are firmly grounded in a specific discipline.
4. I take this title from a line in Salman Rushdie's essay "In Good Faith" which I originally read in Jeremy Waldron's 1991 article "Minority Cultures and the Cosmopolitan Alternative." *University of Michigan Journal of Law Reform* 25: 751–92.

References

Bauböck, Rainer. 2010. Cold Constellations and Hot Identities: Political Theory Questions About Transnationalism and Diaspora. In *Diaspora and Transnationalism: Concepts, Theories and Methods*, ed. Rainer Bauböck and Thomas Faist, 295–321. Amsterdam: Amsterdam University Press.

Brettell, Caroline, and James Frank Hollifield, eds. 2008. *Migration Theory: Talking Across Disciplines*. 2nd ed. New York: Routledge.

Carens, Joseph H. 1987. Aliens and Citizens: The Case for Open Borders. *Review of Politics* 49 (2): 251–273.

Carens, Joseph H. 1992. Migration and Morality: A Liberal Egalitarian Perspective. In *Free Movement: Ethical Issues in the Transnational Migration of People and of Money*, 25–47. University Park, PA: The Pennsylvania State University Press.

Cole, Phillip. 2000. *Philosophies of Exclusion: Liberal Political Theory and Immigration*. Edinburgh: Edinburgh University Press.

Walzer, Michael. 1983. *Spheres of Justice: A Defense of Pluralism and Equality*. New York, NY: Basic Books.

Wimmer, Andreas, and Nina Glick Schiller. 2002. Methodological Nationalism and Beyond: Nation-State Building, Migration and the Social Sciences. *Global Networks* 2 (4): 301–334.

Acknowledgments

I have benefited from comments and conversations with many colleagues on these topics over the years. They include Oliviero Angeli, Rainer Bauböck, Esma Baycan, Elizabeth Brake, Chris Bertram, Michael Blake, Andreas Cassee, Phillip Cole, Jocelyne Couture, Speranta Dumitru, Josiah McC Heyman, Janet Flor Juanico Cruz, Avery Kolers, Patti Tamara Lenard, Matthew Lister, Dennis McKerlie, José Jorge Mendoza, Kai Nielsen, Parvati Raghuram, Amy Reed-Sandoval, Stephanie Silverman, Christine Straehle, Georgiana Turculet, Sara De Vido, Andrew Valls, David Watkins, Shelley Wilcox, and Yusuf Yuksekdag. I apologize in advance to anyone whom I have omitted.

I owe more than I can express to my parents who have read (and edited!) more pages on the political philosophy of migration than they could have imagined when I set off to university to pursue an English literature degree. I am also grateful to my daughter Becky who has put up with my spending too many evening and weekends in front of my laptop; *eres una fuente de luz y alegría. Finalmente, agradezco a Marifer por su apoyo y amor. Los últimos dieciocho años han sido un gran viaje y este libro no hubiera sido posible sin ti.*

Contents

1 Introduction   1

2 Political Philosophy, Migration, and Methodological Nationalism   17

3 Breaking the Nation-State's Spell   37

4 Sites, Systems, and Agents   53

5 Critical Cosmopolitanism and the Ethics of Mobility   69

6 Toward a Political Philosophy of Mobility   91

References   97

Index   99

CHAPTER 1

Introduction

Abstract The bias of methodological nationalism has distorted how people understand migration. Methodological nationalists imagine the world as a set of homogenous societies bounded by impermeable national borders. Mobility within state territories is mostly unremarked, whereas mobility across international borders is seen as pathological. In recent decades, social scientists have mounted formidable criticism of these biases, but political philosophy has not assimilated them. This chapter argues that political philosophers need to become aware of how the nation-building has affected the categories that we use to understand the world and to recognize the many ways that sub-, supra-, and transnational borders affect mobility. This task requires breaking down disciplinary silos and recognizing that mobility is a normal and laudable feature of the world.

Keywords Cosmopolitanism • Methodological nationalism • Mobility • Migration • Political philosophy • Sedentariness

In *Moving Europeans*, historian Leslie Page Moch recounts the trajectory of Joseph Mayett who

> left his parents' Buckingham cottage northwest of London in 1795 at age 12, when his father, a farm laborer, hired him out to be "in service." The young man ate, slept, and resided with his masters since service was paid in

room, board, and a wage. ... Both Mayett and his parents tacitly expected him to be a farm servant, to be hired by the year, and to move annually. Neither party anticipated that he would again live at home, and he did not, except for one short period when he was forced to take work as a farm laborer and find shelter with his parents. Mayett took 11 positions as a farmhand in eight years, sometimes returning to a former master, and never once living more than 23 kilometers from his parents' cottage. (Moch 1992: 22)

Against the myth of a sedentary pre-industrial Europe where peasants put deep roots into national soils, Moch demonstrates that Mayett was in no way atypical: mobility was the norm for the seventeenth century in which "about 65 percent of men and women departed their home parish" (Moch 1992: 23).

Moch's history of mobility in Europe is important and fascinating, but not surprising. Humans are a mobile species—our ancestors moved out of Africa to Eurasia and Australia over 40,000 years ago and have not stopped moving. As the demographer Massimo Livi Bacci states, "territorial movement is a human prerogative and an integral part of human capital; it is one of many ways that the human species has sought to improve its living conditions" (2012: viii). Though the word "migrant" is not always used, the history of the world is very much a history of people moving due to climate change, conquest, slavery, economic opportunity, and wanderlust. Migrants have been a source of goods, ideas, and customs. Despite the best efforts of nationalists to deny the multicultural fabric of their lives, the history of the world is cosmopolitan.

Mobility today is ubiquitous. Today there are an estimated 244 million international migrants (2015 figures) (IOM 2016) and possibly 740 million internal migrants (2009 figures) (UNDP 2009). In 2015, 1186 million international tourists supported a $US 1260 billion industry (UNWTO 2016). Mobility is integral to economies and communities, as well as to the lives of individuals and families. At the same time, it is often stigmatized and the freedom to travel is unevenly distributed. Some people move with ease, while others are forced to remain or to move clandestinely. In many cases, mobility restrictions are accomplished through blunt and violent means such as armed border guards and barbed wire fences. But even more frequently, mobility is shaped in more subtle, insidious ways such as when some groups are extended housing loans with generous terms while others are denied access to credit (Massey 2007) or when gentrification drives populations out of neighborhoods they have occupied for decades. Barriers to mobility can be physical (e.g., walls and jail cells), legal (e.g., prohibitions against migration, against trespassing, or wearing headscarves in public places), and economic (e.g., social policies that make many parts of cities inaccessible to much of the population). They can also be cognitive or symbolic (e.g., people do not know how to access resources or believe [perhaps rightly] that they are not welcome). They can also be unofficial and even illegal, as when members of minorities are treated with suspicion or hostility or given pretexts (e.g., rental requirements that give landlords leeway to refuse to rent to members of some groups) to prevent them from moving into some neighborhoods.

This book is a philosophical investigation of the categories and presuppositions that influence how we think about mobility and migration. My goal is to provide tools for thinking ethically about when enclosure and exclusion have moral warrant and when they should be resisted. This requires a diagnosis of the cognitive biases and schema that shape how we think about mobility, affecting when we notice it (e.g., immigration of the global poor), when it is mostly invisible (e.g., internal mobility between cities in the same national territory), when it is welcomed (e.g., highly skilled workers or "expats" from privileged states), and when it is treated as pathological (e.g., racialized minorities fleeing persecution).

Conceptual analysis of categories and presuppositions helps dispel common misconceptions about migration that misinform political debates and much of the normative literature, especially in political philosophy and political theory. In particular, theorists have analyzed migration from the perspective of the nation-state—and in most of these cases, from the perspective of developed, Western nation-states. This perspective is heavily influenced by the cognitive bias of methodological nationalism (Sager 2016).[1]

Methodological nationalism connects to a sedentarian bias in which movement is ignored or treated as abnormal. Much state-funded social science asks why people move with the implicit or explicit agenda of figuring out how to prevent them from moving—at least into wealthy states. Movement is conceived as a problem; if many people move, it is deemed a crisis. As Nicholas De Genova puts it:

> The Migration Question thus gets transposed into the Migrant Question, and it is indeed around this "problem" that much of the academic research on migration has itself been fundamentally constituted. The very categories of thought that commonly frame discourses of migration, including scholarly

discourses, tend to present migrant mobility as a definite sort of "problem" that implicitly threatens the presumed normative good of "social cohesion" and commands various formulae for enhancing the processes for the "inclusion" of Migrant "outsiders", or perhaps for compelling those "foreigners" to figure out how to appropriately "integrate" themselves. (De Genova 2016: 345)

The sedentarian bias thus treats migration as an unfortunate response to poverty or to violence that should be prevented if possible. Governments have erected walls, intercepted ships, built detention centers, restricted criteria for asylum, and partnered with foreign governments to keep people in their place (De Genova and Peutz 2010). These approaches frame migration as a security issue threatening the well-being, values, and physical security of affluent communities (Feldman 2012). More subtly, the sedentarian bias has supported misguided policy proposals such as coupling development aid with stricter border controls aimed at keeping people at home. Immobility, on these proposals, is achieved by addressing the "root cause" of migration, thought to be largely poverty. This ignores how development and migration are not substitutes, but rather interact: international migration—at least over the short run—*increases* with development (OECD 2016: 115–122).

Attempting to think about migration without the biases of methodological nationalism and sedentarism can be disorienting. It becomes much harder to determine the nature and location of borders since they cannot be treated as synonymous with proclaimed national borders. Also, it introduces complexity to the categorization of migrants which cannot uncritically follow taxonomies imposed by states. Dichotomies imposed by nation-states such as "internal vs. international," "permanent vs. temporary," "legal vs. illegal," "voluntary vs. involuntary" become blurred and less important for empirical and normative thought (King 2002: 92–94).

In recent decades, scholars have begun to overcome the bias of methodological nationalism and to show how mobility is integral to our social, economic, and cultural lives. An ethics of mobility beyond methodological nationalism needs to bring normative theories of migration into contact with this scholarship. Attention to the mobility turn and the critique of methodological nationalism demands more careful attention to the nature of borders and their effects. What this reveals is that an understanding of migration in which borders are treated as invisible lines delimiting state sovereignty is based on an incomplete and mistaken view of the world. Not only have state borders been "externalized"—enforced at distant locations such as airports in different continents, international waters, or foreign territories—they have also become increasingly "internalized" and mobile with surveillance and enforcement occurring in the heartland of national territories. A more perspicuous understanding of borders has implications for normative theory: it suggests that our normative orientation should be a nuanced, critical cosmopolitanism that is sensitive to place and to ways groups of people are subject to hierarchy and segmentation on multiple scales (local, national, regional, global).

SEDENTARISM AND THE CRITIQUE OF METHODOLOGICAL NATIONALISM

Much social science assumes stasis as the default condition (Cresswell 2006; Nail 2015: 3; Sheller and Urry 2006: 212). Movement is seen as secondary to stasis—when it is seen at all. One consequence of the sedentarian bias is that much movement and migration is not even noted. Workers who commute—even when they spend hours of their day travelling—are seen as immobile, as are many internal migrants relocating within state boundaries. Someone who travels 46 miles to work from Las Cruces to El Paso is not considered a migrant; someone who travels seven miles from Cuidad Juarez is.

Sedentarism prevents us from understanding the world which is not static. As Thomas Nail remarks, "Sedentarism, however, is misunderstood as the lack of movement. Sedentarism is not immobility. It is the redirection of social flows, the creation of junctions, and the maintenance of social circulation" (Nail 2015: 39). We filter out mobility and impose stasis in order to categorize and to measure. As long as we recognize this is what we are doing, this is not necessarily problematic—simplification and omission are necessary to comprehend the world. The danger is when we come to forget mobility and confuse representation with reality.

Under sedentarist assumptions, migration is reduced to movement from one fixed point (e.g., a "sending" country) to another (e.g., a "receiving" country). As a result, attention is focused on admission to a political community, rather than the journey itself and the role it plays in the larger context of individuals' lives. People are treated either as citizens or foreigners, compatriots or strangers, ignoring the complexities of identity and the diverse ways in which place and space shape us.

Sedentarism is accompanied by normative judgments under which movement is treated as pathological. Nomadism is treated as an aberration, something chosen temporarily in the quest for stasis or out of necessity. Movement is routinely criminalized and groups such as the Roma and UK Travellers are victims of hate crime and persecution (Fekete 2014; James 2014). James C. Scott notes:

> Aristotle thought famously that man was by nature a citizen of a city (*polis*); people who chose consciously to not belong to such a community (*apolis*) were, by definition, of no worth. When whole peoples, such as pastoralists, gypsies, swidden cultivators follow, by choice, an itinerant or semi-itinerant livelihood, they are seen as a collective threat and are collectively stigmatized. (Scott 2009: 101–102; c.f. Scott 2017)

Sedentarism is closely related to the cognitive bias of methodological nationalism (Sager 2016). Methodological nationalism takes—often unconsciously—the perspective of the state, presupposing a conception of society bounded by impermeable national borders (Beck 2000; Wimmer and Glick Schiller 2002). Since most statistical data is gathered at the state level for state purposes, methodological nationalism is built into the foundation of much social science. This filters out transnational social and economic phenomena that need to be reconstructed from state-centered data sets or go uninvestigated.

Methodological nationalism has also prevented theorists from drawing connections between barriers to mobility between states and barriers to mobility within states and cities. International border regimes prevent people from seeking safety and from accessing opportunities; within states, public space is increasingly privatized and securitized so that it can only be enjoyed by the privileged few (Harvey 2013). Nor is the line between international and internal mobility clear. In many cases, mobility restrictions on migrants continue within state territories as they find that their ethnicity or their legal and economic status confines them to or excludes them from neighborhoods and public spaces.

The biases of sedentarism and methodological nationalism preclude more radical criticisms of migration policy, leading normative theorists to work within the assumptions and categories set by the state. Joseph Carens and David Miller, who in many ways occupy opposite ends of the liberal spectrum on migration, concur that normative recommendations are unrealistic if they fail to assume states' right to exercise considerable discretion over how many people to admit (Carens 2013; Miller 2016). As a result, theorists use state categories that classify migrants and—to borrow a phrase from Catherine Dauvergne (2008)—make people illegal. Instead of questioning the legitimacy of political and legal decisions that create "illegal" status (Bauder 2014), philosophical discussion of "amnesty" has tended to presuppose immigrant wrongdoing and ask about the appropriateness of continuing to exclude long-term residents from the political community (Bosniak 2013; Carens 2010). This in turn reifies the state and its power over populations.

In response, we need to harness other categories and vocabularies. Migration justice is in part an epistemic and semantic task: political philosophers need to inquire into the production of knowledge, how power and interests have shaped dominant categories, and to propose alternative ways of thinking. Otherwise, attempts to reimagine migration policies will remain captive to what are considered politically feasible reforms—for example, increased temporary work visas and legalization of some unauthorized migrants combined with additional enforcement efforts—or will be deemed unfeasible or utopia. The rejection of sedentarism and methodological nationalism calls for new theoretical resources to understand migration and mobility. Research on the mobility turn and in critical border studies provides some of these resources.

Some Resources: Mobility Turn, Transnationalism, and Critical Border Studies

In recent years, an increasing number of social scientists have begun to work in the "new mobilities paradigm" or the "mobility turn" (Cresswell 2010; Urry 2007). Researchers contributing to this "mobility turn" have criticized how social science has privileged stasis. They seek not only to study mobility, but also how it interacts with immobile infrastructures (Sheller and Urry 2006: 212). The capacity to move is supported by roads, airports, and factories producing vehicles for transportation. Movement is also regulated by laws and enforced by agencies that hinder or facilitate it.

The mobilities paradigm brings awareness to how technology has facilitated mobility for some people while imposing restrictions on mobility for others. The ability to travel freely is unevenly distributed (Cresswell 2010: 21). This is true about movement across national borders and also within nation-states. Undocumented status restricts where and how people can live and travel out of fear of detention and deportation and by preventing access to goods—for example, in many places, illegalized immigrants are barred from acquiring a driver's license. It also restricts opportunities, confining people to the shadow economy and limiting their ability to afford to live in many neighborhoods or to access public spaces (e.g., illegalized immigrants, even if allowed admission to universities, may have to pay prohibitively high out-of-state tuition). Internal migration controls affect not only immigrants—they also restrict movement and opportunities for long-term residents and citizens, especially for members of racialized groups identified as "immigrants" (Kukathas 2015; Mendoza 2015).

Mobility is intimately connected with borders. Border studies has moved away from a static conception of borders as lines demarcating the political boundaries of states to finding borders and boundaries virtually everywhere (Johnson et al. 2011). Borders are filters that exclude some and include others. Moreover, inclusion is gradated and multidimensional. Some migrants receive the same formal rights as native-born citizens through naturalization. Others enjoy legal residence but are excluded from citizenship. In some countries—especially if they are white and privileged—immigrants may be almost indistinguishable from citizens except for their lack of power to run for office or vote. Still others receive only the temporary right to remain or are bound to employers who control their continued right to reside in the territory. Borders also disenfranchise some *citizens* because of poverty, a criminal record, or their membership in a marginalized group (Gottschalk et al. 2015).

The suggestion that borders exclude citizens may seem odd, but it is common in border studies to recognize that borders are "complex social institutions, which are marked by tensions between practices of border reinforcement and border crossing" (Mezzadra and Neilson 2013: 3–4). As Étienne Balibar has noted, borders have a "polysemic nature" so that "they do not have the same meaning for everyone" (Balibar 2002: 81). They are designed to

> not merely give individuals from different social classes different experiences of the law, the civil administration, the police and elementary rights, such as the freedom of circulation and freedom of enterprise, but actively to *differentiate* between individuals in terms of social class. (Balibar 2002: 81–82)

With reference to what he terms "cosmopolitan borders" Chris Rumford adds:

cosmopolitan borders are not experienced in the same way by everyone, leading to what we might call a "cosmopolitan paradox": that borders are diffused throughout society, differentiated and networked also increases the chance that they are experienced differently by different groups, some of who encounter them as anything but cosmopolitan. (Rumford 2014: 11)

Under this understanding of borders, the simple valence of where inclusion is positive and exclusion is negative does not withstand scrutiny. As Sandro Mazzadra and Brett Neilson observe, "borders are equally devices of inclusion that select and filter people and different forms of circulation in ways no less violent than those deployed in exclusionary measures" (Mezzadra and Neilson 2013: 7). Thomas Nail has pointed out how some borders have a centripetal function that brings the periphery into the center (Nail 2016: 49). Borders are necessary to centralize power and bring people together. This supports an economy capable of generating surpluses and allows for complex societies to emerge. It also allows rulers to tax, conscript, and enslave populations (Scott 2009; Scott 2017).

CRITICAL COSMOPOLITANISM AND AN ETHICS OF MOBILITY

Many normative theorists writing on migration have taken liberal nationalist, communitarian, or statist positions (Blake 2013; Miller 2016; Walzer 1983). My conviction is that an adequate ethics for immigration must be cosmopolitan (Cole 2000; Kukathas 2005),[2] but that moral cosmopolitanism—understood as the view that all human beings have equal moral worth regardless of their political, religious, ethnic, or other membership—is inadequate to orient us on its own. Cosmopolitanism as an ethical stance is too often reduced to a facile acknowledgement of the moral equality of all humans, fully compatible with strong preference to compatriots and a conservative vision of the continued role of nation-states (Scheffler 2001). In the ethics of immigration, David Miller has recently endorsed a "weak cosmopolitan" basis for assessing migration policy in which obligations to non-citizens are limited to a duty to respect their human rights, understood as the rights protecting what people need for "minimally decent lives" (Miller 2016: 31-6). The result is that many moral cosmopolitans have come to see their view as compatible with liberal nationalism and, in some cases, endorse quite restrictive constraints on migration and mobility (Brock 2009; Miller 2016).

Criticisms of methodological nationalism challenge the empirical basis of these positions: sub, supra, and transnational processes and memberships cast doubt on the conceptions of the nation, community, or state that underlie these normative accounts. In the social sciences, critics of methodological nationalism such as Ulrich Beck have advanced cosmopolitanism as a methodological stance for empirical research (Beck 2004). This research reveals how methodological nationalism, by imposing the perspective of the nation-state on how we interpret the world, neglects or distorts cosmopolitan phenomena and practices. The phenomena that nationalist, communitarianism, and statist theorists take to be morally significant are not adequately demarcated by the territories they prioritize.

At the same time, cosmopolitanism features of the world do not map in a straightforward way onto an ethics of open borders. Though I have considerable sympathy for arguments for open borders or no borders (Sager 2017) and believe the burden of proof rests on those who wish to exclude people, there are legitimate reasons for limiting mobility under some circumstances. Borders are not only repressive; they also allow for the creation and preservation of goods that further human flourishing. Borders limit opportunities for some, but they can also make possible opportunities for others.

What is needed is a critical cosmopolitanism (Delanty 2006) that treats barriers to mobility between and within societies based on categories such as class, race, ethnicity, gender, and disability as fundamental to moral analysis. We need to jettison an anemic moral cosmopolitanism in favor of a critical cosmopolitanism that takes structural injustice seriously and addresses it *as* structural injustice. Border controls do not affect all foreigners equally nor do they exhaust how restrictions to mobility circumscribe opportunities. Moreover, mobility is stratified by social class and by people's positions within transnational networks.

The insistence on using the nation-state as the unit of analysis also obscures how mobility restrictions limit access to opportunities within nation-states (e.g., in many major cities, low-wage workers—including immigrants—cannot afford to live near their place of work and must commute for hours every day) (Sassen 2008). One upshot of recognizing how methodological nationalism has distorted thinking on the ethics of migration and of endorsing critical cosmopolitanism is that this illuminates how borders enacting class-stratification, racialization, and sexism affect mobility and access to opportunities *within territories* (e.g., gated communities, segregation within cities) for both migrants and citizens.

In the case of migrants, Rhacel Salazar Parreñas has shown how domestic workers find themselves excluded from both private space—the homes they live and work in—and public space:

> Employers control the spatial movements of domestic workers as they decide on the domestic's integration into or segregation from the family. More often than not, they prefer segregation, as they ... tend to hire those who will demand very few resources in terms of time, money, space, or interaction. ... In both Los Angeles and Rome, Filipina domestics, including nannies and elder-care providers, found themselves subject to food rationing, prevented from sitting on the couch, provided with a separate set of utensils, and told when to get food from the refrigerator and when to retreat to their bedrooms. (Salazar Parreñas 2008: 99)

Migration policy in many countries confines workers to the homes of their employers as a condition for their continued employment where they are vulnerable to abuse.

Mobility restrictions also extend from the domestic sphere to the public sphere. Many immigrant and minority groups are concentrated in "ghettos" in underprivileged city sectors. Salazar Parreñas tells how the Italian police harassed Filipino vendors who gathered around bus stops, forcing the Filipino community to eventually relocate to an underpass by the Tiber River:

> This place of gathering under the bridge has given Filipino migrants in Rome a haven away from the "public domain" yet in the "public domain". Nonetheless, their very presence under the bridge serves as a reminder in the community that they do not belong in the public social space of Italian society. (Salazar Parreñas 2008: 105)

What Salazar Parreñas describes is experienced by many communities that find themselves part of but apart from the larger communities in which they reside.

Moving beyond methodological nationalism brings together topics that are usually discussed separately, allowing us to break down disciplinary silos in normative studies of migration, multiculturalism, and urbanism. It draws connections between mobility across international borders, segregation, gentrification, and the privatization of public space. Instead of debating open and closed state borders, a more fruitful investigation addresses how borders and boundaries exclude people and hinder mobility more generally. This calls for an ethics of mobility where international migration is but one type. Instead of asking whether border controls are permissible or impermissible, an ethics of mobility asks questions such as what are the goods protected by borders and boundaries? Should these goods be protected in this way? Who is excluded from accessing these goods? Why are these people excluded? How are they excluded? What are the means of exclusion, and are they proportional? This introduces considerable complexity into normative debates, but also promises a more comprehensive and realistic account of how we should think ethically about movement.

Structure of Book

The aim of this book is primarily conceptual and critical: it seeks to identify biases in normative writing about migration and to clear the ground for future work unencumbered by methodological nationalism. A primary goal is to identify how *not* to think ethically about migration and mobility and to suggest a more adequate approach. To do this, Chap. 2 describes the cognitive bias of methodological nationalism in more detail and surveys normative work on the ethics of migration to show how much of it has remained within methodological nationalism's clutches. Chapter 3 surveys work in the social sciences that help us shake off the blinders of methodological nationalism. Chapter 4 applies this work to advocate for the relevance of migration systems to the ethics of migration, as well as for the need to give greater attention to mobility barriers within nation-states and cities. It also makes a case for the importance of corporations, non-governmental organizations (NGOs), and other actors for the ethics of mobility. Chapter 5 applies some of these insights to the film *La Haine*. It sketches a cosmopolitan framework for thinking ethically about migration, argues for the need to bring empirical work and political philosophy together, and presents dimensions of an ethics of mobility that can help address structural injustice. The final chapter draws together some of the implications of an ethics of mobility.

Notes

1. The phrase "methodological nationalism" is in some ways unfortunate, given that one of the problems with methodological nationalism is that it has led theorists conflate the nation and the state, ignoring how many states have more than one national community and how many nations inhabit more than one state. Indeed, one of the earlier criticisms of methodological nationalism was made by Anthony Smith who contended that it led to the neglect of *nationalism* in part because social theorists largely treated the nation as a "given" (Smith 1983: 26).

In some respects, "methodological statism" would be a more perspicuous term. Be that as it may, most of the literature refers to methodological nationalism.
2. Joseph Carens' influential writings on the ethics of migration, especially in his recent *Ethics of Immigration* (2013), can be placed in both camps. Sometimes he presupposes an international order of sovereign states with the right to significantly restrict immigration and enquires into the limitations of this right; in other places he argues for open borders using cosmopolitan presuppositions.

References

Balibar, Étienne. 2002. *Politics and the Other Scene*. London: Verso.
Bauder, H. 2014. Why We Should Use the Term 'Illegalized' Refugee or Immigrant: A Commentary. *International Journal of Refugee Law* 26 (3): 327–332.
Beck, Ulrich. 2000. *What Is Globalization?* Cambridge, UK and Malden, MA: Polity Press.
———. 2004. Cosmopolitical Realism: On the Distinction Between Cosmopolitanism in Philosophy and the Social Sciences. *Global Networks* 4 (1): 131–156.
Blake, Michael. 2013. Immigration, Jurisdiction, and Exclusion. *Philosophy & Public Affairs* 41 (2): 103–130.
Bosniak, Linda. 2013. Amnesty in Immigration: Forgetting, Forgiving, Freedom. *Critical Review of International Social and Political Philosophy* 16 (3): 344–365.
Brock, Gillian. 2009. *Global Justice: A Cosmopolitan Account*. Oxford and New York: Oxford University Press.
Carens, Joseph H. 2010. *Immigrants and the Right to Stay*. A Boston Review Book. Cambridge, MA: MIT Press.
———. 2013. *The Ethics of Immigration*. New York: Oxford University Press.
Cole, Phillip. 2000. *Philosophies of Exclusion: Liberal Political Theory and Immigration*. Edinburgh: Edinburgh University Press.
Cresswell, Tim. 2006. *On the Move: Mobility in the Modern Western World*. New York: Routledge.
———. 2010. Towards a Politics of Mobility. *Environment and Planning D: Society and Space* 28 (1): 17–31. https://doi.org/10.1068/d11407.
Dauvergne, Catherine. 2008. *Making People Illegal: What Globalization Means for Migration and Law*. Cambridge and New York: Cambridge University Press.
De Genova, Nicholas. 2016. The 'European' Question: Migration, Race, and Post-Coloniality in 'Europe'. In *An Anthology of Migration and Social Transformation*, ed. Anna Amelina, Kenneth Horvath, and Bruno Meeus, 343–356. Cham: Springer International Publishing.

De Genova, Nicholas, and Nathalie Mae Peutz, eds. 2010. *The Deportation Regime: Sovereignty, Space, and the Freedom of Movement.* Durham, NC: Duke University Press.

Delanty, Gerard. 2006. The Cosmopolitan Imagination: Critical Cosmopolitanism and Social Theory. *The British Journal of Sociology* 57 (1): 25–47.

Fekete, Liz. 2014. Europe Against the Roma. *Race & Class* 55 (3): 60–70.

Feldman, Gregory. 2012. *The Migration Apparatus: Security, Labor, and Policymaking in the European Union.* Stanford, CA: Stanford University Press.

Gottschalk, Marie, Amy E. Lerman, Naomi Murakawa, and Vesla M. Weaver. 2015. Critical Trialogue: The Carceral State. *Perspectives on Politics* 13 (3): 805–8014.

Harvey, David. 2013. *Rebel Cities: From the Right to the City to the Urban Revolution.* Paperback ed. London: Verso.

International Organization for Migration. 2016. 2015 Global Migration Trends 2015 Factsheet. Geneva and Switzerland: International Organization for Migration. https://publications.iom.int/system/files/global_migration_trends_2015_factsheet.pdf

James, Zoë. 2014. Hate Crimes Against Gypsies, Travellers and Roma in Europe. In *The International Handbook of Hate Crime*. London: Routledge.

Johnson, Corey, Reece Jones, Anssi Paasi, Louise Amoore, Alison Mountz, Mark Salter, and Chris Rumford. 2011. Interventions on Rethinking 'the Border' in Border Studies. *Political Geography* 30 (2): 61–69.

King, Russell. 2002. Towards a New Map of European Migration. *International Journal of Population Geography* 8 (2): 89–106. https://doi.org/10.1002/ijpg.246.

Kukathas, Chandran. 2005. The Case for Open Immigration. In *Contemporary Debates in Applied Ethics*, ed. Andrew Cohen and Christopher Heath Wellman, 207–220. Malden, MA: Blackwell.

———. 2015. Why Immigration Controls Resemble Apartheid in Their Adverse Consequences for Freedom. *Democratic Audit UK*, September 15. http://www.democraticaudit.com/2015/09/15/why-immigration-controls-resemble-apartheid-in-their-adverse-consequences-for-freedom/

Livi Bacci, Massimo. 2012. *A Short History of Migration.* Translated by Carl Ipsen. Cambridge, UK and Malden, MA: Polity.

Massey, Douglas S. 2007. *Categorically Unequal: The American Stratification System.* A Russell Sage Foundation Centennial Volume. New York: Russell Sage Foundation.

Mendoza, José Jorge. 2015. Enforcement Matters: Reframing the Philosophical Debate on Immigration. *Journal of Speculative Philosophy* 29 (1): 73–90.

Mezzadra, Sandro, and Brett Neilson. 2013. *Border as Method, or, the Multiplication of Labor.* Durham: Duke University Press.

Miller, David. 2016. *Strangers in Our Midst: The Political Philosophy of Immigration.* Cambridge, MA: Harvard University Press.

Moch, Leslie Page. 1992. *Moving Europeans: Migration in Western Europe Since 1650.* Bloomington and Indianapolis, IN: Indiana University Press.

Nail, Thomas. 2015. *The Figure of the Migrant*. Stanford, CA: Stanford University Press.

———. 2016. *Theory of the Border*. Oxford and New York: Oxford University Press.

OECD. 2016. *Perspectives on Global Development 2017*. Perspectives on Global Development. OECD Publishing. http://www.oecd-ilibrary.org/development/perspectives-on-global-development-2017_persp_glob_dev-2017-en

Rumford, Chris. 2014. 'Seeing Like a Border': Towards Multiperspectivalism. In *Cosmopolitan Borders*, ed. Chris Rumford, 39–54. London: Palgrave Macmillan UK.

Sager, Alex. 2016. Methodological Nationalism, Migration and Political Theory. *Political Studies* 64 (1): 42–59.

———. 2017. Immigration Enforcement and Domination: An Indirect Argument for Much More Open Borders. *Political Research Quarterly* 70 (1): 42–54.

Salazar Parreñas, Rhacel. 2008. *The Force of Domesticity: Filipina Migrants and Globalization*. Nation of Newcomers. New York: New York University Press.

Sassen, Saskia. 2008. Two Stops in Today's New Global Geographies: Shaping Novel Labor Supplies and Employment Regimes. *American Behavioral Scientist* 52 (3): 457–496.

Scheffler, Samuel. 2001. *Boundaries and Allegiances: Problems of Justice and Responsibility in Liberal Thought*. Oxford, UK: Oxford University Press.

Scott, James C. 2009. *The Art of Not Being Governed: An Anarchist History of Upland Southeast Asia*. Yale Agrarian Studies Series. New Haven: Yale University Press.

Scott, James C. 2017. *Against the Grain: A Deep History of the Earliest States*. Yale Agrarian Studies. New Haven: Yale University Press.

Sheller, Mimi, and John Urry. 2006. The New Mobilities Paradigm. *Environment and Planning A* 38 (2): 207–226.

Smith, Anthony D. 1983. Nationalism and Classical Social Theory. *The British Journal of Sociology* 34 (1): 19–38.

United Nations Development Programme. 2009. *2009 Human Development Report 2009—Overcoming Barriers: Human Mobility and Development*. New York, NY: United Nations. http://hdr.undp.org/en/content/human-development-report-2009

United Nations World Tourism Organization. 2016. *UNWTO: Tourism Highlights, 2016 Edition*. Madrid, Spain: World Tourism Organization (UNWTO). http://www.e-unwto.org/doi/pdf/10.18111/9789284418145

Urry, John. 2007. *Mobilities*. Malden, MA: Polity.

Walzer, Michael. 1983. *Spheres of Justice: A Defense of Pluralism and Equality*. New York, NY: Basic Books.

Wimmer, Andreas, and Nina Glick Schiller. 2002. Methodological Nationalism and Beyond: Nation-State Building, Migration and the Social Sciences. *Global Networks* 2 (4): 301–334.

CHAPTER 2

Political Philosophy, Migration, and Methodological Nationalism

Abstract This chapter explains in detail the cognitive bias of methodological nationalism and shows how it has shaped much work in the political philosophy of migration. Methodological nationalism combines the assumptions of sedentariness, state sovereignty, territorial borders, and membership encouraged by nation-building projects. Political philosophers have for the most part assumed that the site of justice is a closed nation-state in which people enter by birth and exit by death. Though in recent years philosophers have begun to shake off the methodological nationalism of their discipline, it remains a powerful influence that has distorted reflection on the ethics of migration and discouraged reflection on forms of exclusion that take place within, outside, and across state territorial borders.

Keywords Methodological nationalism • Political philosophy • Sedentariness • Transnationalism

Political philosophy can awaken us to the strangeness of the world by refusing to take authority as natural or necessary and by demanding justification for institutions and practices that seem natural and inevitable. Rather than accepting relationships of hierarchy, coercion, and inequality as given, it can reveal their contingency and—as is often the case—their perversity. In doing so, it creates the possibility of change by suggesting that things could be otherwise.

Unfortunately, political philosophers have mostly failed to fully come to terms with how migration and mobility challenge many of the fundamental assumptions of their discipline. They have analyzed it using categories that distort its nature, thereby failing to adequately account for its complexity. As a result, how we think ethically about migration is not adequately informed by how its nature, prompting a need to reconsider our fundamental political categories and to reassess our questions and conclusions about the ethics of migration.

The dominant tradition in Anglo-American political philosophy from Hobbes' *Leviathan* to John Rawls' *Theory of Justice* (1999a) has taken the state as its unit of analysis. Rawls—who set the agenda for much Anglo-American political philosophy in the last quarter of the twentieth century—proceeded from the assumption of a closed society in which people enter society by birth and exit by death (Rawls 1993: xiv). Though he later supplemented his account of justice for closed societies in *Theory of Justice* and *Political Liberalism* (1993) with the international ethics of *The Law of Peoples* (1999b), his unit of analysis remained autonomous, independent societies.[1]

Over the last 30 years, political philosophers have called into question many of Rawls' fundamental assumptions. Feminist, multicultural, indigenous, and critical race perspectives have challenged the cogency of conceiving justice in terms of "social cooperation among equals for mutual advantage" (Rawls 1999b: 13), showing how this can serve to obscure internal diversity, conflict, and systemic oppression and exploitation. Normative studies of nationalism have forced theorists to distinguish nation and state and to take into account minority national groups. Cosmopolitans have questioned the moral significance of the state and the national community and redefined the scope of justice. Historically informed scholarship has explored the role of imperialism and colonialism in nation-building and emphasized how imperial and colonial projects have fostered uneven development.

One way of describing these developments is that political philosophers have been chipping away at the edifice of methodological nationalism that has dominated their field. Methodological nationalism is a cognitive bias in which researchers take the nation-state as their unit of analysis (Dumitru 2014: 9; c.f. Chernilo 2011). Criticisms of methodological nationalism emerged in sociology in the 1970s with Hermínio Martins' observation that macro-sociology had largely accepted the national community as "the terminal unit and boundary condition for the demarcation of problems and phenomena for social sciences" (Martins 1974: 276).[2] Anthony Smith noted the failure of classical sociological theory to theorize nationalism, treating nations and nationalism as a "sociological 'given'"—a practice which includes collecting social data within a nationalist frame (Smith 1983: 26).

Methodological nationalism gained widespread attention with the rise of globalization theory, most prominently through the work of Ulrich Beck (2000, 2002). Beck writes:

> Globality means that the unity of national state and national society comes unstuck; new relations of power and competition, conflict and intersection, take shape between, on the one hand, national states and actors, and on the other hand, transnational actors, identities, social spaces, situations and processes. (Beck 2000: 21)

Though jubilation over the nation-state's supposed demise and of globalization's alleged novelty has been tempered in recent decades, debates about globalization have made clear the need to reevaluate methods and categories. Rejecting methodological nationalism does not mean we need to endorse extravagant claims about how globalization has transformed the world in unprecedented ways. It does entail moving beyond methodological nationalism when theorizing the role of the state and nation. Our theories, if they are not to suffer from incompleteness and inaccuracy, must find a way to account for "transnational actors, identities, social spaces, situations, and processes."

One might imagine that migration studies would be less vulnerable to methodological nationalism. Migration is by definition transnational—to study immigration independently of emigration is to not study *migration* at all (Jacobson 2006). Too often scholarship and policy treats the "immigrant" as a figure without history, unconnected to any other place other than the country of settlement, miraculously transplanted into a national community to which it must "integrate." Furthermore, it is difficult to reconcile national mythology with migration history. Migrants disrupt nation-building projects premised on fixed communities that share language, culture, and history and draw attention to how imaginary communities were consciously, as well as imperfectly, constructed.

Despite the seeming incongruity between a nationalist view of the world and serious migration scholarship, Andreas Wimmer and Nina Glick Schiller have shown that methodological nationalism has infected migration studies, leading researchers to ignore the nation-state, to naturalize it, or to analyze migration within its territorial limit: "Describing immigrants as political security risks, as culturally others, as socially marginal, and as an exception to the rule of territorial confinement, migration studies have faithfully mirrored the nationalist image of normal life" (Wimmer and Glick Schiller 2003: 599; c.f. Wimmer and Glick Schiller 2002). Migration studies colluded in nation-building projects, ignoring the historical processes that led to the nation-state and providing models in which ethnic groups' assimilation or integration is defined by their perceived distance from the allegedly homogenous national community.

Bringing these observations together, we can understand the cognitive bias of methodological nationalism as a set of features characterizing an idealized political society. Though not all of the features of methodological nationalism occur simultaneously, they are closely related. They include conceptions of sovereignty, borders and boundaries, membership, and mobility.[3]

First, the bias of methodological nationalism assumes sedentariness. Wimmer and Glick Schiller write: "in the eyes of nation-state builders and social scientists alike, every move across national frontiers becomes an exception to the rule of sedentariness within the boundaries of the nation-state" (Wimmer and Glick Schiller 2003: 585). Migration is treated as abnormal and in need of justification despite the 244 million international migrants (IOM 2016) and 1186 million tourists (UNWTO 2016) in 2015, along with a substantially larger population within states whose parents or grandparents migrated.

A by-product of sedentariness is that internal migration becomes largely invisible. Methodological nationalism treats the mobility of people within the boundaries of the state as irrelevant or categorizes it as urbanization (in which the focus is not on movement itself, but the end result of people migrating). As a result, internal migration remains understudied and its connections to international migration have been neglected (King and Skeldon 2010).

Second, methodological nationalism presupposes that state sovereignty is unified. States are considered the primary political actor, possessing supreme authority within their territorial boundaries, including the right and the power to regulate cross border flows of goods, capital, and people. This ignores the ways in which treaties, conventions, and human rights norms affect state rights and underemphasizes the limits of state capacity to prevent mobility. It also overlooks the ways in which other states frequently exercise de jure and de facto control over foreign territories (Krasner 1999). Furthermore, it omits how sub-state actors, including minority national groups and cities, legitimately exercise power, sometimes in opposition to state-level policies and preferences (Sassen 2008).

Third, people befuddled by methodological nationalism reduce borders to territorial borders which are in turn seen as fixed and immutable. One effect of this presupposition is to treat nation-states as autonomous systems governed by their own laws whose scope ends at the frontier. In migration studies, this is embedded in explanations of human mobility in terms of "pushes" and "pulls." Emigrants are "pushed" out of their societies because of limited opportunities or violence; they are "pulled" to other societies because of these societies' wealth and democratic institutions. Push/pull explanations ignore the connections that link sending and receiving states, fail to explain why people move from a particular region to another, and efface transnational spaces.

The focus on state borders has also led to the neglect of how internal borders and boundaries restrict and regulate migration. Borders are highly mobile, appearing wherever they are recognized and enforced (Shachar 2009b). Much immigration enforcement takes place within states through raids and detention centers, as well as through cooperation with law enforcement, private employers, and landlords, as well as other government agencies. In the United States, Customs and Border Protection (CBP) has extensive powers to search vehicles and to detain people within 100 air miles of any external boundary. The popular perception is that CBP enforcement is limited to the border and to designated checkpoints miles away from the US-Mexico border. In fact, two-thirds of the US population live within a "Constitution-Free Zone"—so-dubbed by the American Civil Liberties Union (ACLU) because of the limited protection of the Constitutional right against unreasonable search and seizure (ACLU n.d.).

Internal borders in the European Union have also increasingly dispelled the illusion of free movement between member states. Austria, Bulgaria, Hungary, Macedonia, and Slovenia have built barriers to prevent migration into their territories. France and the United Kingdom have also constructed a barrier to prevent migrants from accessing the Channel Tunnel. Though these barriers resonate symbolically with anti-immigrant nationalists and cause migrants misery by making their travel more difficult (and often more expensive), they do not appear to stop migration. Regarding the erection of new border barriers by Hungary on the Serbian border, Wendy Brown observes that "these barriers do not repel but divert migration flows coming from the east and south, and they also now link to a system channeling migrants through the Balkans and into the heart of Europe. This in turn converts whole nations into European borders, corridors rather than destinations" (Jones et al. 2017: 3).

Border enforcement has also been externalized in complex ways (Boswell 2003; Collyer and King 2015; Gibney 2006; Nessel 2009). In fact, most migration enforcement does not take place at official state borders. Borders are often established by state and private patrols policing international waters or located in airports thousands of miles away from the territory. Or they are created by foreign police or soldiers paid to stop emigration and to turn back transit migrants hoping to breach Europe's fortress (Andersson 2014). Sometimes admissions are determined by immigration offices abroad. More often, people are turned away by airlines that face heavy sanctions if they allow unauthorized passengers to embark. Though these borders are often not recognized as borders, they are no less—and often more—effective in immobilizing migrants or diverting them toward alternative, often dangerous routes.

Fourth, methodological nationalism presupposes that states have fixed membership in which each person fully belongs to one (and only one) country. This ignores dual citizenship, transnational families and communities, sub-state political communities (which in some cases enjoy substantial autonomy), long-term permanent residents without citizenship, temporary residents, as well as people who for a variety of reasons lack the legal status to remain on the territory. Furthermore, under methodological nationalism, theorists presuppose a culturally homogenous society in which the presence of ethnic minorities is treated as an anomaly that will eventually be assimilated. Departures from the dominant culture as defined by nation-building projects are seen as problematic and vaguely threatening. Stephen Castles notes how sociology and anthropology colluded with Western nation-states in colonial projects: social, cultural, and economic knowledge served to control "dangerous classes" and "dangerous peoples"—industrial workers and colonial subjects (Castles 2007: 356). One result is that strangers came to be seen as deviant and potentially dangerous; migrants needed "to undergo a process of 'acculturation' to renounce their original culture and adopt the values, norms and behavior of the receiving society" (Castles 2007: 356).

Empirical researchers and normative theorists have largely approached political reality through the methodologically nationalist prism of political society. They filter out features in the world not included in the model defined by methodological nationalism. Similarly, they ignore or distort processes that the model does not capture. Nobody believes that the world exactly mimics these features, but most social scientists and political philosophers beguiled by methodological nationalism believe that it fits them closely enough. Exceptions are dealt with in an ad hoc manner, if they are acknowledged at all.

In the next chapter, I will say more about how social scientists have challenged and begun to move beyond methodological nationalism and what this means for normative theory. In what remains of this chapter, I want to show that the political philosophy of migration has been operated within the clutches of methodological nationalism.

The Political Philosophy of Migration

Given how the social sciences have been closely intertwined with the rise of the nation-state, it should not be surprising that political philosophy has also legitimized and reified the methodological nationalist view of the world. In particular, social contract theory from Hobbes to Rawls has presupposed a homogenous, unified community formed by individuals who come together to establish a state.[4] Social contract theory with its ahistorical, depersonalized contractors eliminates the messiness and complexity of real societies and real politics in favor of an idealization that tends to confirm the prejudices of those in power.

One would expect that attention to migration as a normative issue would force political philosophy to renounce methodological nationalism. Migration dispels—or should dispel—any illusion of a homogenous population, raising the issue of dual and multiple political memberships. The presence of long-term residents without citizenship, temporary residents, and people without the legal authorization to live in the territory invite us to rethink our conception of citizenship. Furthermore, arguments for mobility rights challenge the legitimacy of nation-states' attempts to curtail movement across their borders. The "turbulence of migration" (Papastergiadis 2000) challenges states' ability to do so. Though states exercise considerable power over migrants, they are far from being able to control them. Indeed, the lengths that states go to prevent migration flows, often entering into repugnant agreements with authoritarian regimes and private contractors (United Nations Support Mission in Libya 2016), suggest the limits of classical conceptions of state sovereignty.

Nonetheless, political philosophy, even when it is advocating open borders, has remained very much within the framework imposed by methodological nationalism (Sager 2016b). To make broad claims about trends in a discipline—in this case political philosophy—is risky business. There are invariably exceptions to any generalization and one inevitably neglects the nuances of many accounts. At the same time, without generalizations, we risk getting caught up in particularities and lose the opportunity to make a case for shifting the direction of research in the field.[5] By and large, the conception of society and state defined by methodological nationalism has defined normative discussion. Political philosophy has left the state system more or less intact and failed to recognize how profoundly migration disrupts dominant political categories.

The surge in writing on migration in mainstream political philosophy over the last three decades is largely due to Joseph Carens' "Aliens and Citizens: The Case for Open Borders" (1987).[6] Before then, political philosophers had largely overlooked migration. Insofar as they thought about the topic at all, they mostly took for granted state discretion over admissions policy. Carens observed that "borders have guards and guards have guns" (251), signaling how migration is restricted (often with appalling violence [Jones 2016]). He pointed out that three major political theories—Rawlsian egalitarianism, Nozickian libertarianism, and utilitarianism—all seemed to support open borders. If we assume that people's life chances should not be determined by their place of birth, insist on the fundamental right to free movement and to engage in voluntary transactions, or care about well-being, then it is hard to justify immigration restrictions.

The importance of Carens' article lies not only in its defense of open borders (which has been vigorously contested), but also in the way that it opened an area of inquiry that had been previously neglected with potentially radical consequences. In particular, Phillip Cole fruitfully used migration to delve into the conceptual foundations of liberalism, noting the asymmetry between the widely endorsed right to emigrate and the widely supported right of states to prevent immigration (Cole 2000; Wellman and Cole 2011).[7] On Cole's account, we need to overcome this asymmetry and, by doing so, reimagine our account of political membership and borders (Wellman and Cole 2011: 301–303).

Nonetheless, the case for open borders left many of the assumptions of methodological nationalism intact. The response to Carens—including some ways in which Carens himself developed his views over the next

25 years[8]—was surprisingly conservative. Theorists quickly mustered the claims of communities, nations, property owners, and others to defend state rights to restrict immigration. Many of these arguments started from a particular conception of the nation-state, characterized by shared political culture (Miller 2005), political association (Wellman 2008), or jurisdiction (Blake 2013). Paradoxically, some theorists argued that fulfilling cosmopolitan obligations of global justice require *restricting* immigration (Brock 2009; Christiano 2008).

My purpose is not to weigh in on these debates here, but rather to show that even defenses of open borders usually leave much of the state system intact.[9] The critical attention to borders is salutary, but it does not go far enough. Methodological nationalism continues to dominate normative work in political philosophy, at least in the Anglo-American analytic tradition, as we continue to uncritically accept states' self-definitions and categories.[10] The ethics of immigration, despite its many challenges to the status quo, remains in fundamental ways a victim of this ideology. It has taken place against a distorted understanding of the world that in turn contributes to reinforcing the state system. Even open-borders advocates' continued focus on state borders reinforces the notion of homogenous, unified political communities, despite their rejection of these communities' right to control admissions.

The very fact that immigration has become a topic in political philosophy relies on the bias of sedentariness. Immigration has shifted from being invisible to theorists to being a problem. Both the invisibility and the problematization of immigration occur because of the assumption of stasis. By and large, movement has been characterized as pathological, something to be undertaken only with great necessity. Even arguments for more open borders based on inequalities caused by place of birth treat immigration as an anomaly, something that would not occur at significant levels without economic disparities (Carens 1992; Shachar 2009a). This has led to defenses of border controls that hinge on allowing affluent countries to discharge any obligations to ameliorate inequities, human rights violations, and other wrongs through development aid or humanitarian intervention, rather than admitting migrants (Pevnick 2011; Wellman and Cole 2011; Miller 2016). These authors remain undeterred by the fact that migration in fact tends to *increase* as people become more affluent (Castles 2008; Clemens 2014; Haas 2007; UNDP 2009). Transnational lives and networks, despite being longstanding and widespread, are not treated as part of the fabric of our societies, but are rather seen—if they are seen at all—as abnormal violations of the imperative that people remain fixed to the state's territory.

A further reason to believe that methodological nationalism has infected political philosophy is the discipline's overwhelming focus on the ethics of *immigration* rather than on *migration*. Joseph Carens' *The Ethics of Immigration* (2013), Peter Higgin's *Immigration Justice* (2013), Ryan Pevnick's *Immigration and the Constraints of Justice* (2011), and Christopher Heath Wellman and Philip Cole's exchange *Debating the Ethics of Immigration* (2011) are all primarily about immigration.[11] This is also true of Phillip Cole's *Philosophies of Exclusion* (2000) (subtitled *Liberal Political Theory and Immigration*) and David Miller's *Strangers in Our Midst* (2016) (subtitled *The Political Philosophy of Immigration*). Survey articles by Blake (2005), Seglow (2005), and Wellman (2015) are also on *immigration*. Sarah Fine and Lea Ypi's recent collection *Migration in Political Theory* (2016) at first glance appears to buck the trend, but upon closer examination most of the contributions turn out to be on immigration.

In fact, the focus in political philosophy is even narrower. Most publications only tackle the question of whether affluent, Western democracies have obligations to admit immigrants for settlement. The false (Eurocentric) assumption is that the main reason people migrate is the opportunity to join more affluent, well-governed Western societies. This ignores how on most metrics South-South migration (37% of total international migrant stock) exceeds South-North migration (35% of total international migrant stock) (IOM 2016).[12]

To characterize migration in terms of immigration and settlement neglects circular migration, transit migration, and migrants who have transnational lives spanning two or more territories. Though temporary migration has received some attention from political philosophers, the debate has largely taken place against the backdrop of settlement—is it just to provide temporary admission for work without providing a pathway for workers to eventually acquire permanent membership and citizenship?[13] The focus has also been on migration to North America (excluding Mexico), Western Europe, and Australasia with restrictive policies in the Middle East, Hong Kong, and Singapore treated as models of injustice to be rejected or reluctantly tolerated under current political realities (Carens 2008; Ruhs 2013). Political philosophers have also neglected what Leo Lucassen and Aniek Smit (2015) dub "organizational migrants"—soldiers, missionaries, and aid workers. The result is that everyone is either a member of a state or in the process of attempting to become a member of a new state. Under this definition migration is necessarily a temporary and usually undesirable state—the nomad, rover, and peripatetic are anomalies that can be safely ignored.

When *emigration* has been brought into the picture, it has largely been around the discussion of "brain drain"—the emigration of skilled workers from less to more developed countries (Brock and Blake 2015).[14] The "brain drain" debate treats migration as a zero-sum game between sending and receiving territories seeking to gain or retain human capital and pits the rights and interests of would-be emigrants against the states or national communities they wish to leave. This debate only makes sense under the thrall of methodological nationalism (Sager 2016c).

Another effect of framing the discussion around *immigration* is that it makes it easier to overlook internal migration. This includes the migration of residents and citizens to cities as the world urbanizes and the expulsion of less affluent long-term residents from many city neighborhoods. It also neglects the internal dimensions of immigration policy where immigrants—those with the legal right to be present in the territory and those without—are often subject to detention and deportation, as well as widespread restrictions in their access to housing, social services, drivers' licenses, and much else. These policies affect racialized minority citizens along with immigrants, revealing how the boundaries of belonging frequently blur.

Political philosophers have also assumed a notion of sovereignty based on methodological nationalism. States exert considerable—often lethal (IOM 2016)—influence over migration flows—but the notion of a closed border is a fiction that resembles neither today's world nor any world that has ever existed. Often debates on immigration restrictions are centered around the presumed commitments of liberal states—respect for fundamental freedoms or for principles of anti-racism or non-discrimination is leveraged to show limits to how liberal states may treat immigrants (Blake 2013; Carens 2013). This debate assumes that these state policies are endogenous, based on their internal legal and normative regimes, overlooking the ways that these regimes are structured by international treaties and foreign policy (FitzGerald and Cook-Martin 2014). State discretion and hence sovereignty over the right to control immigration is always constrained.

When we move from the right to determine immigration policy to the capacity to exert control over migration flows, states are even less effective.

Saskia Sassen has long emphasized the role of non-state and inter- and transnational processes in causing and shaping migration flows (Sassen 1999). These include multinational corporations, international organizations such as the International Monetary Fund, foreign direct investment, and trade agreements, as well as military intervention. It also includes migration itself which in many cases self-perpetuates through the acts of individual migrants and social networks, regardless of attempts to restrict it (Papadopoulos and Tsianos 2013).

To be sure, state policies and bureaucracies do channel and divert migration flows, but the ability of states to control migration is always limited and often counterproductive. In many cases, the effect of restrictions is to make immigration more costly, both by creating an industry for smugglers to move people clandestinely across borders and by increasing the risk of death and injury for migrants (Sanchez 2015). Paradoxically, in some countries such as the United States, immigration restrictions actually caused a rise in the undocumented population, both through the "illegalization" of people (Bauder 2014) who formerly enjoyed the right to be on the territory and by ending circular migration (and consequently causing settlement through increasing the cost of exiting and returning to the country) (Massey et al. 2016). Wendy Brown probably overstated in *Walled States, Waning Sovereignty* (2010) the extent to which sovereignty has in fact diminished in recent years, but her thesis that border walls are mainly acts of political theater rather than effective means of actually stopping migration remains cogent (as the election of Donald Trump around the slogan of building a wall and making Mexico pay for it confirms) (Jones et al. 2017).

Sedentariness and a constricted conception of sovereignty combine with a container model of state and society (in which society is thought to correspond to state). Under methodological nationalism, borders are seen to be fixed rather than continuously constructed. This helps explain the attraction for proposals to substitute development aid for the obligation to admit poor people into wealthier countries, despite the knowledge that development *increases* mobility. The blithe tendency to conflate official development aid with accepting migration (usually with little effort to establish that they could in fact be substitutes) makes sense only if we see states as self-contained systems.

Much work in political philosophy assumes that membership remains within state territories. Community is assumed to be something that exists within territorial boundaries, overlooking diaspora and other transnational connections (Bauböck and Faist 2010). Arguments for restricting immigration based on freedom of association, cultural preservation, or self-determination rarely ask whether the community or culture that holds these rights or interests is in fact contained within state boundaries (Miller 2005; Wellman 2008). When it becomes apparent that not everybody in the territory is a citizen, the debate turns to culture, particularly questions about the need for supposedly liberal polities to tolerate allegedly illiberal cultures (Carens 2013; Miller 2016; Orgad 2015).[15]

Furthermore, political philosophers and theorists have seen the ethics of mobility as a question about the right to cross national borders. This ignores the many forms of exclusion and expulsion that take place within states and outside of territorial borders. Much of the discussion concerns integration: what are the obligations of states to grant full membership to non-citizens or regularize the status of unauthorized immigrants (Carens 2013)? Far less attention has been given to deportation, detention, and raids.[16] Political philosophers have also largely failed to engage the literature in the social sciences and law on the externalization of border controls (Sager 2017). The result is that methodologically nationalist political philosophy fails to recognize the reality of migration and the effect of internal and external enforcement on migrants and the many people connected to them.

Conclusion

The purpose of this chapter has been to describe the cognitive bias of methodological nationalism and show how much work in the political philosophy of migration has been beholden to it. In the next chapter, I turn to how social scientists have sought to go beyond methodological nationalism through increased attention to mobility, transnationalism, and the nature of borders. New categories open up new normative questions, connect areas of philosophy such as the ethics of migration and philosophy of the city, and help guide us to a more adequate approach to the topic that eschews methodological nationalism.

Notes

1. Indeed, Rawls almost entirely neglects the topic of immigration, suggesting that once the major causes of immigration—persecution, the denial of human rights, starvation, and population pressure—are removed, immigration ceases to be an issue for political philosophy: "The problem of immigration is not, then, simply left aside, but is eliminated as a serious problem in a realistic utopia" (Rawls 1999b: 9).

2. Though he did not explicitly use the term "methodological nationalism," Anthony Giddens also deserves recognition as an early critic of methodological nationalist tendencies (Giddens 1973: 265; c.f. Chernilo 2011; Dumitru 2014).
3. In identifying these features I draw on a paper by Speranta Dumitru (2014) that identifies three versions of methodological nationalism: state-centrism (in which the nation-state is taken as the primary and most important unit of analysis), territorialism (in which space is defined by national territories), and groupism (in which society is equated with the nation-state).
4. As Carole Pateman's *The Sexual Contract* (1988) and Charles W. Mill's *The Racial Contract* (1997) reveal, the metaphors and narratives of social contract theory have always had an exclusionary function and an ideological effect that enables readers to ignore or oppress those not party to the contract.
5. For my analysis, I draw on my reading of some of the most influential monographs, edited collections, and survey articles on the ethics of migration, including Barry and Goodin (1992), Blake (2005), Carens (2013), Cole (2000), Fine and Ypi (2016), Higgins (2013), Miller (2016), Pevnick (2011), Seglow (2005), Wellman and Cole (2011), and Wellman (2015).
6. The other "founding" text in the ethics of immigration is arguably Michael Walzer's chapter on membership in *Spheres of Justice* (1983). Ackerman (1980) and Nett (1971) in some respects anticipated Carens' arguments, but neither received widespread attention.
7. Ann Dummett (1992: 173) anticipated Cole's point about the need for symmetry between immigration and emigration.
8. In most of the chapter in *The Ethics of Immigration*, Carens assumes that states are morally entitled to considerable discretion over the admission of immigrants.
9. I present my position on the open border debate in Sager (2017).
10. Matters are somewhat different in the continental tradition influenced by Agamben, Delueze and Guattari, and Foucault—Thomas Nail's important work (2015, 2016) comes to mind. This tradition exerts more influence in disciplines outside of philosophy.
11. I confess that this generalization also holds for my own edited collection *The Ethics and Politics of Immigration: Core Issues and Emerging Trends* (2016a).
12. Anthony Smith connected sociology's Eurocentrism to its neglect of nationalism, noting that sociology "arose, after all, in countries with a fairly firmly entrenched sense of nationality, which was both clear-cut and dominant within the state apparatus and polity" (Smith 1983: 25). This led theorists to take nationalism for granted and instead to focus on socioeconomic structures rather than the evolution of nationalism.

13. For a sample of work on temporary migration, see Carens (2008), Lenard and Straehle (2011), Ottonelli and Torresi (2012), and Ruhs (2013).
14. Michael Clemens (2009) has advocated for replacing the pejorative hydraulic metaphor of "brain drain" with the more neutral "skill flow." I concur (with the caveat that skill flow ask risks dehumanizing migrants by reducing them to human capital), but the phrase "brain drain" has unfortunately remained entrenched.
15. See Volpp (2000) and (2001) for valuable discussion of how anti-social behavior by native-born citizens identified with the majority is considered to be deviant, whereas similar types of behavior by groups identified as cultural minorities are treated as symptomatic of their cultural norms.
16. These topics have only recently begun to receive attention. On immigration enforcement, see Mendoza (2015) and Sager (2017); on immigrant detention, see Silverman (2016); and on deportation, see Lenard (2015).

REFERENCES

Ackerman, Bruce A. 1980. *Social Justice in a Liberal State*. New Haven: Yale University Press.
Andersson, Ruben. 2014. *Illegality, Inc.: Clandestine Migration and the Business of Bordering Europe*. California Series in Public Anthropology 28. Oakland, CA: University of California Press.
Barry, Brian, and Robert E. Goodin, eds. 1992. *Free Movement: Ethical Issues in the Transnational Migration of People and Money*. University Park, Pennsylvania: Pennsylvania State University Press.
Bauböck, Rainer, and Thomas Faist, eds. 2010. *A Global Perspective on Transnational Migration: Theorizing Migration Without Methodological Nationalism*. Amsterdam: Amsterdam University Press.
Bauder, H. 2014. Why We Should Use the Term 'Illegalized' Refugee or Immigrant: A Commentary. *International Journal of Refugee Law* 26 (3): 327–332.
Beck, Ulrich. 2000. *What Is Globalization?* Cambridge, UK and Malden, MA: Polity Press.
Beck, U. 2002. The Cosmopolitan Society and Its Enemies. *Theory, Culture & Society* 19 (1–2): 17–44.
Blake, Michael. 2005. Immigration. In *Blackwell Companion to Applied Ethics*, ed. Christopher Heath Wellman and R.G. Frey, 224–237. Oxford: Blackwell Publishers.
———. 2013. Immigration, Jurisdiction, and Exclusion. *Philosophy & Public Affairs* 41 (2): 103–130.
Boswell, Christina. 2003. The 'External Dimension' of EU Immigration and Asylum Policy. *International Affairs* 79 (3): 619–638.

Brock, Gillian. 2009. *Global Justice: A Cosmopolitan Account*. Oxford and New York: Oxford University Press.
Brock, Gillian, and Michael Blake. 2015. *Debating Brain Drain: May Governments Restrict Emigration?* New York, NY: Oxford University Press.
Brown, Wendy. 2010. *Walled States, Waning Sovereignty*. New York and Cambridge, MA: Zone Books and Distributed by the MIT Press.
Carens, Joseph H. 1987. Aliens and Citizens: The Case for Open Borders. *Review of Politics* 49 (2): 251–273.
———. 1992. Migration and Morality: A Liberal Egalitarian Perspective. In *Free Movement: Ethical Issues in the Transnational Migration of People and of Money*, 25–47. University Park, Pennsylvania: The Pennsylvania State University Press.
Carens, Joseph. 2008. Live-in Domestics, Seasonal Workers, and Others Hard to Locate on the Map of Democracy. *Journal of Political Philosophy* 16 (4): 429–445.
———. 2013. *The Ethics of Immigration*. New York: Oxford University Press.
Castles, Stephen. 2007. Twenty-First-Century Migration as a Challenge to Sociology. *Journal of Ethnic and Migration Studies* 33 (3): 351–371.
———. 2008. Development and Migration—Migration and Development: What Comes First? In *Migration and Development: Further Directions for Research and Policy*, 10–32. http://essays.ssrc.org/developmentpapers/wp-content/uploads/MigrationDevelopmentSSRCConferencePapers.pdf.
Chernilo, Daniel. 2011. The Critique of Methodological Nationalism: Theory and History. *Thesis Eleven* 106 (1): 98–117.
Christiano, T. 2008. Immigration, Political Community and Cosmopolitanism. *San Diego Law Review* 45: 933–961.
Clemens, Michael. 2009. *Skill Flow: A Fundamental Reconsideration of Skilled-Worker Mobility and Development*. Working Paper 180, Center for Global Development CGD, Washington, DC.
Clemens, Michael A. 2014. Does Development Reduce Migration? In *International Handbook on Migration and Economic Development*, ed. Robert E.B. Lucas, 152–185. Elgar Original Reference. Cheltenham, UK: Edward Elgar.
Cole, Phillip. 2000. *Philosophies of Exclusion: Liberal Political Theory and Immigration*. Edinburgh: Edinburgh University Press.
Collyer, Michael, and Russell King. 2015. Producing Transnational Space: International Migration and the Extra-Territorial Reach of State Power. *Progress in Human Geography* 39 (2): 185–204.
Dumitru, Speranta. 2014. Qu'est-Ce Que Le Nationalisme Methodologique? *Raisons Politiques* 52: 9–22.
Dummett, Ann. 1992. The Transnational Migration of People Seen from Within a Natural Law Tradition. In *Free Movement: Ethical Issues in the Transnational Migration of People and of Money*, 169–180. University Park, Pennsylvania: The Pennsylvania State University Press.

Fine, Sarah, and Lea Ypi, eds. 2016. *Migration in Political Theory: The Ethics of Movement and Membership.* 1st ed. Oxford, UK: Oxford University Press.

FitzGerald, David, and David Cook-Martín. 2014. *Culling the Masses: The Democratic Origins of Racist Immigration Policy in the Americas.* Cambridge, MA: Harvard University Press.

Gibney, Matthew. 2006. A Thousand Little Guantanamos: Western States and Measures to Prevent the Arrival of Refugees. In *Displacement, Asylum, Migration: The Oxford Amnesty Lectures 2004,* ed. Kate E. Tunstall, 139–169. Oxford and New York: Oxford University Press.

Giddens, Anthony. 1973. *The Class Structure of the Advanced Societies.* London: Hutchinson.

de Haas, Hein. 2007. Turning the Tide? Why Development Will Not Stop Migration. *Development and Change* 38 (5): 819–841.

Higgins, Peter. 2013. *Immigration Justice.* Edinburgh: Edinburgh University Press.

International Organization for Migration. 2016. 2015 Global Migration Trends 2015 Factsheet. Geneva and Switzerland: International Organization for Migration. https://publications.iom.int/system/files/global_migration_trends_2015_factsheet.pdf

Jacobson, Matthew Frye. 2006. More 'Trans-,' Less 'National'. *Journal of American Ethnic History* 25 (4): 74–84.

Jones, Reece. 2016. *Violent Borders: Refugees and the Right to Move.* London and New York: Verso.

Jones, Reece, Corey Johnson, Wendy Brown, Gabriel Popescu, Polly Pallister-Wilkins, Alison Mountz, and Emily Gilbert. 2017. Interventions on the State of Sovereignty at the Border. *Political Geography* 59 (July): 1–10. https://doi.org/10.1016/j.polgeo.2017.02.006.

King, Russell, and Ronald Skeldon. 2010. 'Mind the Gap!' Integrating Approaches to Internal and International Migration. *Journal of Ethnic and Migration Studies* 36 (10): 1619–1646.

Krasner, Stephen D. 1999. *Sovereignty: Organized Hypocrisy.* Princeton, NJ: Princeton University Press.

Lenard, P.T. 2015. The Ethics of Deportation in Liberal Democratic States. *European Journal of Political Theory* 14 (4): 464–480.

Lenard, P.T., and C. Straehle. 2011. Temporary Labour Migration, Global Redistribution, and Democratic Justice. *Politics, Philosophy & Economics* 11 (2): 206–230.

Lucassen, Leo, and Aniek X. Smit. 2015. The Repugnant Other: Soldiers, Missionaries, and Aid Workers as Organization Migrants. *Journal of World History* 26 (1): 1–39.

Martins, Herminio. 1974. Time and Theory in Sociology. In *Approaches to Sociology: An Introduction to Major Trends in British Sociology,* ed. J. Rex, 246–294. London: Routledge & Kegan.

Massey, Douglas S., Jorge Durand, and Karen A. Pren. 2016. Why Border Enforcement Backfired. *American Journal of Sociology* 121 (5): 1557–1600.

Mendoza, José Jorge. 2015. Enforcement Matters: Reframing the Philosophical Debate on Immigration. *Journal of Speculative Philosophy* 29 (1): 73–90.

Miller, David. 2005. Immigration: The Case for Limits. In *Contemporary Debates in Applied Ethics*, ed. Andrew Cohen and Christopher Heath Wellman, 193–206. Malden, MA: Blackwell.

———. 2016. *Strangers in Our Midst: The Political Philosophy of Immigration*. Cambridge, MA: Harvard University Press.

Mills, Charles W. 1997. *The Racial Contract*. Ithaca and London: Cornell University Press.

Nail, Thomas. 2015. *The Figure of the Migrant*. Stanford, CA: Stanford University Press.

———. 2016. *Theory of the Border*. Oxford and New York: Oxford University Press.

Nessel, Lori A. 2009. Externalized Borders and the Invisible Refugee. *Columbia Human Rights Law Review* 40 (625): 625–699.

Nett, Roger. 1971. The Civil Right We Are Not Ready For: The Right of Free Movement of People on the Face of the Earth. *Ethics* 81 (3): 212–227.

Orgad, Liav. 2015. *The Cultural Defense of Nations: A Liberal Theory of Majority Rights*. New York, NY: Oxford University Press.

Ottonelli, Valeria, and Tiziana Torresi. 2012. Inclusivist Egalitarian Liberalism and Temporary Migration: A Dilemma. *Journal of Political Philosophy* 20 (2): 202–224.

Papadopoulos, Dimitris, and Vassilis S. Tsianos. 2013. After Citizenship: Autonomy of Migration, Organisational Ontology and Mobile Commons. *Citizenship Studies* 17 (2): 178–196.

Papastergiadis, Nicholas. 2000. *The Turbulence of Migration*. Cambridge: Polity.

Pateman, Carole. 1988. *The Sexual Contract*. Stanford, CA: Stanford University Press.

Pevnick, Ryan. 2011. *Immigration and the Constraints of Justice: Between Open Borders and Absolute Sovereignty*. Cambridge and New York: Cambridge University Press.

Rawls, John. 1993. *Political Liberalism*. Expanded ed. Columbia Classics in Philosophy. New York: Columbia University Press.

———. 1999a. *Theory of Justice: Revised Edition*. Cambridge, MA: Harvard University Press.

———. 1999b. *The Law of Peoples*. Cambridge, MA: Harvard University Press.

Ruhs, Martin. 2013. *The Price of Rights: Regulating International Labor Migration*. Princeton, NJ: Princeton University Press.

Sager, Alex., ed. 2016a. *The Ethics and Politics of Immigration: Core Issues and Emerging Trends*. Lanham: Rowman & Littlefield International.

———. 2016b. Methodological Nationalism, Migration and Political Theory. *Political Studies* 64 (1): 42–59.

———. 2016c. Methodological Nationalism and the 'Brain Drain'. In *The Ethics and Politics of Immigration: Core Issues and Emerging Trends*, ed. Alex Sager. Lanham: Rowman & Littlefield International.

———. 2017. Immigration Enforcement and Domination: An Indirect Argument for Much More Open Borders. *Political Research Quarterly* 70 (1): 42–54.

Sanchez, Gabriella E.2015. *Human Smuggling and Border Crossings*. Routledge Studies in Criminal Justice, Borders and Citizenship. London and New York, NY: Routledge.

Sassen, Saskia. 1999. *Guests and Aliens*. New York, NY: New Press.

———. 2008. Two Stops in Today's New Global Geographies: Shaping Novel Labor Supplies and Employment Regimes. *American Behavioral Scientist* 52 (3): 457–496.

Seglow, Jonathan. 2005. The Ethics of Immigration. *Political Studies Review* 3 (3): 317–334.

Shachar, Ayelet. 2009a. *The Birthright Lottery: Citizenship and Global Inequality*. Cambridge, MA: Harvard University Press.

———. 2009b. The Shifting Border of Immigration Regulation. *Michigan Journal of International Law* 30 (3): 165–193.

Silverman, Stephanie J. 2016. The Difference That Detention Makes: Reconceptualizing the Boundaries of the Normative Debate on Immigration Control. In *The Ethics and Politics of Immigration: Core Issues and Emerging Trends*, ed. Alex Sager. Lanham: Rowman & Littlefield International.

Smith, Anthony D. 1983. Nationalism and Classical Social Theory. *The British Journal of Sociology* 34 (1): 19–38.

United Nations Development Programme. 2009. *2009 Human Development Report 2009—Overcoming Barriers: Human Mobility and Development*. New York, NY: United Nations. http://hdr.undp.org/en/content/human-development-report-2009

United Nations Support Mission in Libya. 2016. *Detained and Dehumanised: Report on Human Rights Abuses Against Migrants in Libya*. United Nations Human Rights. https://unsmil.unmissions.org/Portals/unsmil/Documents/Migrants%20report-EN.pdf

United Nations World Tourism Organization. 2016. *UNWTO: Tourism Highlights, 2016 Edition*. Madrid, Spain: World Tourism Organization (UNWTO). http://www.e-unwto.org/doi/pdf/10.18111/9789284418145

Volpp, Leti. 2000. Blaming Culture for Bad Behavior. *Yale Journal of Law & the Humanities* 12 (1): 89–116.

———. 2001. Feminism Versus Multiculturalism. *Columbia Law Review* 101 (5): 1181–1218.

Wellman, Christopher Heath. 2008. Immigration and Freedom of Association. *Ethics* 119 (1): 109–141.

———. 2015. Immigration. Edited by Edward N. Zalta. *The Stanford Encyclopedia of Philosophy.* https://plato.stanford.edu/archives/sum2015/entries/immigration/

Wellman, Christopher Heath, and Phillip Cole. 2011. *Debating the Ethics of Immigration: Is There a Right to Exclude?* Debating Ethics. Oxford: Oxford University Press.

Wimmer, Andreas, and Nina Glick Schiller. 2002. Methodological Nationalism and Beyond: Nation-State Building, Migration and the Social Sciences. *Global Networks* 2 (4): 301–334.

Wimmer, Andres, and Nina Glick Schiller. 2003. Methodological Nationalism, the Social Sciences, and the Study of Migration: An Essay in Historical Epistemology. *International Migration Review* 37 (3): 576–610.

CHAPTER 3

Breaking the Nation-State's Spell

Abstract Once the bias of methodological nationalism is recognized, the next step is to describe the world in ways that do not unduly privilege the nation-state. This chapter offers resources from the social sciences that help us to break the spell of methodological nationalism. It surveys scholarship in transnational history, transnationalism, mobility, and border studies that provides categories other than the nation-state that play a decisive role in understanding migration. This literature provides a richer and more diverse account of borders that has normative implications which have not received sufficient attention among normative theorists.

Keywords Border studies • Methodological nationalism • Migration history • Mobility • Transnationalism

So far my aim has been primarily diagnostic and critical. I have sought to establish that normative work on migration has been distorted by the cognitive bias of methodological nationalism. But while criticisms of methodological nationalism serve to clear the ground and to draw attention to our presuppositions, they are of limited value if they do not serve as a prelude to alternative ways of looking at the world. As Stephen Castles remarks, "If the dynamics of social relations transcend borders, then so must the theories and methods used to study them" (Castles 2007: 355).

© The Author(s) 2018
A. Sager, *Toward a Cosmopolitan Ethics of Mobility*,
Mobility & Politics, https://doi.org/10.1007/978-3-319-65759-2_3

Political philosophers should take inspiration from social scientists who have begun to transcend methodological nationalism. In this chapter, my goal is to explore categories and conceptions that help us go beyond methodological nationalism. This will lay the groundwork for normative theory that escapes the confines of a world defined by the nation-state.

Cosmopolitan Social Science

A first step in moving beyond methodological nationalism is to recognize that the nation-state is neither natural nor inevitable (Malešević 2017). State monopolization of the authority to restrict movement is a recent development. The nation-state arguably only established itself as the dominant form of political organization in the twentieth century. The capacity to regulate movement depends on the rise of bureaucracy and technologies necessary to reliably identify people. Identification documents only became firmly established by the end of the nineteenth century (Torpey 1998: 242). Before the rise of the modern state system, much of the authority to regulate movement rested in the hands of private entities such as landlords and slaveholders. This is not to endorse returning the authority to control movement to private entities—let alone to countenance feudalism, slavery, or indentured servitude. Rather, it is to insist that there is nothing necessary about state monopoly of migration control.[1]

One way of overcoming methodological nationalism is to consciously assume another perspective. Transnational history projects such as Italian Workers around the World (Gabaccia and Ottanelli 2005) help dispel many of the myths that have resulted from nationalist history. Donna Gabaccia describes

> two different agendas inherent in transnational history. One is to reject the tyranny of the national by seeking alternative concepts and alternative scales for writing history above, below, within, or outside individual nations—whether as global or regional histories. The other is to use transnational history to critique national historiographies from the outside and to insist that historians of particular nations recognize how histories focused on nation building distort the past. (Gabaccia 1999: 1123)

Conducting world history around diaspora and internationalism helps dispel the immigration paradigm that has informed nationalist historiography and social science. When we reject the nationalist perspective that sees

Italians as "immigrants" who joined the United States' "melting pot" and instead assume the migrants' point of view, a number of things become apparent. Italy was not even a country before 1861 and before 1920 few "Italian" migrants spoke Italian. Many identified "l'America" with any destination outside of Italy and saw the United States as just another destination (in fact, during much of this period it was not considered a particularly attractive one). Of the 27 million "Italians" who left "Italy" for the Americas, Australia, Africa, and other European destinations between 1789 and the 1970s, many had no intention of settling and later returned home.

History helps us think beyond and outside of the nation-state. Political theorists have also offered their own resources. Erik Ringmar has observed an "anti-nomadic bias" in political theory (Ringmar forthcoming). Political theorists have identified the nomad with the barbarian, the uncivilized, or the primitive in ways that not only misrepresent nomadic societies, but also foment state ideology. State propagandists juxtapose migrants with sedentary populations, identifying them as an unruly enemy and praising the virtues of the city and empire (Scott 2017).

Consciously assuming the perspective of the migrant or the nomad has proven fruitful. Deleuze and Guattari's "nomadology" explores how the nomadic "war machine" at different points in history conquered cities and empires (1987: 394), demonstrating how unsustainable it is to imagine nomads as ignorant of technology and lacking in organization. Influenced by Deleuze and Guattari, Thomas Nail provocatively asks, "What would it mean to rethink political theory based on the figure of the migrant rather than on citizenship?" (Nail 2015: 18). Nail sees much of history and social science as defining the migrant "according to the dominant type of social order from which it is expelled" (Nail 2015: 15).

One upshot of Nail's analysis is it makes explicit how migration often results from expulsion because of the expansion of state institutions and capital. Nail understands expulsion as not only forcing people off their land, but also depriving them of their political and social rights—including by enslaving them (Nail 2015: 23). Nail notes: "The social conditions for the expansion of a growing political order (including warfare, colonialism, and massive public works) were precisely the expulsion of a population of barbarians who had to be depoliticized at the same time" (Nail 2015: 22). This shift in perspective has significant consequences for normative theory: instead of seeing migrants as anomalies attempting to encroach on state authority, it draws attention to how states violently compel people to move. As Saskia Sassen (2014) demonstrates, expulsions through capital investment, financialization, environmental degradation, and mass incarceration continue apace.

These analyses have much in common with James C. Scott's *The Art of Not Being Governed* (2009) on groups in Zomia (a 2.5 million square kilometer region covering highlands in Southeast, East, and South Asia) that are not incorporated into the state. Scott's thesis is that these groups are best understood as consciously evading states, rather than as primitive, pre-modern societies. They resist taxation, conscription, forced labor, and slavery by creating communities and technologies aimed at resisting the encroachment of state administrations:

> Most, if not all, of the characteristics that appear to stigmatize hill peoples—their location at the margins, their physical mobility, their swidden agriculture, their flexible social structure, their religious heterodoxy, their egalitarianism, and even the nonliterate, oral cultures—far from being the mark of primitives left behind by civilization, are better seen on a long view as adaptations designed to evade both state capture and state formation. (Scott 2009: 9)

A change of perspective can support a research program. In fact, it has led to a number of research programs (or perhaps more accurately, beginnings of such programs) to serve as a counterpoint to methodological nationalism. Ulrich Beck's cosmopolitan social science seeks to understand global risks such as climate change and terrorism (Beck 2004). It also attempts to capture inequalities invisible to analyses that rely on statistics compiled by nation-states and to acknowledge the "banal cosmopolitanism" that increasingly informs many people's lives.[2] Gerard Delanty has developed a "critical cosmopolitanism" that seeks to understand how social reality is changing in ways that are not reducible to either globalization or nationalism (Delanty 2009). Cosmopolitan imagination connects cosmopolitanism as a normative theory, an experience of reality, and a critical attitude aimed toward emancipation through openness, interaction, and the overcoming of divisions (Delanty 2012).

None of these approaches endorse a simplistic shift from the national to the cosmopolitan or universal. One reason for this is that "cosmopolitan" is very much (perhaps essentially) a contested concept (Gallie 1955; Connolly 1993). It comes in various forms: as a moral vision or attitude, as a research program that aims at better describing and explaining twenty-first-century reality, as a set of institutional proposals, or as a form of critical theory. Cosmopolitanism can range from the simple recognition of the moral worth of all humans that is fully compatible with the nation-state system (Miller 2016; Nussbaum 2007) to ambitious claims that political and social reality has been fundamentally and irrevocably transformed, demanding new forms of governance (Held 1995).

Most cosmopolitan research programs do not deny the continued role of nation-states or suggest that the world has suddenly become "flat" (Friedman 2005). Place continues to matter, though the ability to connect distant physical spaces electronically and to rapidly travel the globe has changed its nature in many cases (Harvey 1989). Many examples of "globalization" are best conceived not as cosmopolitan, but as transnational processes that are territorial bound and local, as well as geographically dispersed. People stratified by class, race, gender, and other categories also experience these processes differently—transnationalism connects people but it can also exclude. Globalization usually falls short of encompassing the globe and access to technology remains unevenly distributed.

Nonetheless, the lives of many people are in an important sense banally cosmopolitan. Cosmopolitan research at its best insists that understanding globalization and social transformation means moving beyond methodological nationalism and acknowledging complex connections on many levels—including how groups and regions are differentially affected or excluded from global trends. This orientation is critical *and* constructive: critical in questioning the adequacy of explanations structured by methodological nationalism, constructive in seeking more adequate frames and tools.

Though a developed cosmopolitan research program that could serve as an alternative to the nationalist research programs that define the social sciences still eludes us, many specific research programs have begun to replace nationalist social science. In particular, increased attention to mobility as a research topic, work on transnationalism and plural membership, and attempts to theorize borders open up vistas for thinking normatively about migration.

Research on Mobility, Transnationalism, and Borders

One prejudice of methodological nationalism (and of the social sciences more widely) is sedentarism. Social science has tended to neglect or to minimize the extent to which people's lives and goals depend on mobility, as well as to overlook the transportation infrastructure necessary to make much of everyday life possible (Urry 2007: 19). Research on mobility seeks to remove this prejudice by naturalizing movement and by acknowledging its central place in most social and economic processes (Salazar 2017: 6). Work, school, and leisure depend on transportation and communication systems that shape and enable our experiences and opportunities. The mobility turn seeks to show how immobile structures are integrated with and depend extensively on movement (Sheller and Urry 2006). It does not celebrate mobility for its own sake or disparage stasis, but rather draws attention to their complex interactions. For example, factories are geographical bound, but they are linked in supply chains that bring together commodities, capital, and workers, often spanning continents.

Sheller and Urry stress how place and technology "enhance the mobility of some peoples and places *and* heighten the immobility of others, especially as they try to cross borders" (Sheller and Urry 2006: 207). This includes legal regimes which allow for a ranking of passports—according to one index, first-ranked Germany allows visa-free travel to 159 countries, whereas Afghanistan permits visa-free travel to only 23.[3] By showing how the capacity to move and how access to goods and capitals are central to our social life and well-being, research on mobility ties directly to normative questions about inequality and privilege.

Another facet of methodological nationalism is the identification of society with the state. People are seen as "belonging" to one and only one state. Furthermore, they are abstractly conceived as citizens of this state, enjoying full membership rights. But as the discussion of the Italian Workers around the World project illustrates, immigration is necessarily transnational and ties to countries of origin do not dissolve at the border. Historians, as well as anthropologists, sociologists, and geographers have traced the ways in which many people's lives occur in spaces that cannot be reduced to national territories.

The label of "transnationalism" describes ways in which social, political, and economic processes cut across state barriers. The model of sovereignty posited by methodological nationalism has never described the world (Krasner 1999: 223). Nonetheless, national governments today are immersed in cross-border economic, political, legal, and cultural regimes that they have neither the power nor authority to control (Held 1999). Transnationalism gained prominence in international relations as theorists began to reflect on the role of transnational processes in shaping world politics and the behavior of states (Keohane and Nye 1972). In law, scholars have increasingly explored how human rights norms guide and constrain national governments with national courts increasingly crossing borders to draw on foreign courts for guidance (Slaughter 2005). Sociologists have argued that world-society models explain many of the features of nation-state, including culture, structure, and behavior (Meyer et al. 1997), and have revealed how international non-governmental organizations (INGOs) establish and reinforce world-cultural principles (Boli and Thomas 1997). Democratic theorists have noted how political movements are often international, as demonstrated by the World Social Forum where activists from around the world meet yearly as a counterpart to the World Economic Forum in Davos.

Of particular interest for our purposes is research on migrant transnationalism. The fieldwork of anthropologists such as Linda Basch, Nina Glick Schiller, and Cristina Szanton Blanc contended that many immigrants are better understood as "transmigrants": "people whose daily lives depend on multiple and constant interconnections across international borders and whose public identities are configured in relationship to more than one nation-state" (Glick Schiller et al. 1995). Transmigrants are embedded in networks that span multiple countries, allowing them to respond to shifts in global economic processes. In some cases, households send members abroad as a strategy to offset risk (Stark 1991).

Transnational migration brings more than economic and cultural interaction. In many cases, people abroad have fostered social and political movements, opposing colonial rule or organizing against dictatorships (Glick Schiller et al. 1995: 56–9). Transnational political activity isn't restricted to sub-state actors seeking to contest state power. As Michael Collyer and Russell King point out, "the state inevitably tries to reterritorialize transnational and diasporic spaces" (Collyer and King 2015: 186). In fact, one factor in promoting transnational identity has been nation-building in which states seek to mobilize citizens abroad and benefit from their economic contributions (including remittances). Countries with large transnational populations such as China, India, Mexico, the Philippines, Morocco, and Turkey maintain economic and political ties.

Political scientists and political theorists have become increasingly aware of how mobility disrupts conceptions of membership and citizenship developed around nation-building projects (Bauböck and Faist 2010). In recognition of many people's multiple membership and allegiances, many countries tolerate or embrace dual citizenship (Faist and

Gerdes 2008). A total of 115 countries extend voting rights to citizens abroad (Ellis et al. 2007). Chris Rumford observes:

> The changing spatiality of politics—represented by, for example, the emergence of supra-national governance (for example, the EU), networks of global cities, and transnational communities of fate—means that political space can no longer be equated with that of the nation-state, and, as a consequence, bordering processes have undergone concomitant changes, acquiring a spatiality beyond territoriality. (Rumford 2006: 160)

At the same time, people connected to more than one territory often lack full political and social recognition and rights. Citizenship is complex and multidimensional, combining legal, political, and cultural aspects. People living in state territories have a variety of legal statuses, ranging from full political and social rights to exclusion from the franchise, exclusion from permanent residence, and lack of legal rights to reside in the territory (Cohen 2009). Social status also matters. Even with legal entitlements, many people—including in many places women and racial and ethnic minorities—are unable to exercise their political rights (Young 2011). Today many people still consider the native-born children and grandchildren of migrants to be "immigrants" in their country of birth.

Political trans*nationalism* in many of its forms (e.g., extraterritorial voting rights) still preserves the idea that people are connected to discrete territories, even if their activities span borders. Any adequate theory of globalization needs to explain how territory continues to matter. Nonetheless, people's territorial connections in some cases are contingent and fungible. This is most evident in Dimitris Papadopoulos and Vassilis Tsianos' notion of a mobile commons brought into existence through the dispersed cooperation of migrants. They define the mobile commons as

> the innumerable uncoordinated but cooperative actions of mobile people that contribute to its making. People on the move create a world of knowledge, of information, of tricks for survival, of mutual care, of social relations, of services exchange, of solidarity and sociability that can be shared, used and where people contribute to sustain and expand it. (Papadopoulos and Tsianos 2013: 190, quoted in King 2016: 34)

The relationship of this commons to territory is ephemeral, appearing and dissolving as people arrive, interact, and take their leave.

So far I have discussed how research has sought to dispel the bias of sedentariness and show the importance of transnational connections and processes in explaining the world. Another tendency of methodological nationalism is to conceive the nation-state in terms of its external borders. Transnationalism already does much to dispel this "territorial trap" (Agnew 1994). In their survey article on transnational migration studies, Peggy Levitt and B. Nadya Jawrsky point out:

> In the light of contemporary globalization, scholars acknowledge that the sanctity of border and boundaries is a very recent development, both in human history and in social scientific theory. They also recognize that humans continually create and recreate boundaries, moving, trading, and communicating across them, thereby making fluidity and change a part of all human social formations and processes. (Levitt and Jaworsky 2007: 146)

This brings us to border studies which goes still further in examining the ways in which humans "create and recreate boundaries" by exploring the implications of what Chris Rumford calls "seeing like a border" (Rumford 2014a, b). Border studies denaturalizes and dispels the inevitability of borders by drawing attention to how they are constructed.

Migration controls have fluctuated between openness and exclusion in response to economic and political tension and ideological manipulation (Fassin 2011: 216). Élisabeth Vallet and Charles-Philippe David have documented the rise of border walls from 1945 to 2010. In 1945, there were only five border walls in the world. States built 19 walls and barriers between 1945 and 1991. After the fall of the Berlin wall, they added seven more walls from 1991 to 2001. States completed or planned an additional 28 walls after 9/11 (Vallet and David 2012: 113). This trend has continued to accelerate in recent decades, bringing the total of walls in 2016 to nearly 70 (Jones 2016).

Border walls are political theater with significant symbolic force (Brown 2010). Their role in containing migration is much more ambiguous (Jones 2016). In practice, border walls often divert migration into more dangerous routes, create a market for networks of smugglers, and replace circular migration with settlement by raising the pecuniary and human costs of migrating (Massey et al. 2016).

Border studies reveals how narrow much of the debate about borders has been. Walls are only one sort of barrier or boundary.[4] Nonetheless, normative work on immigration has tended to assume that ethical analysis primarily concerns entrance to the states' external borders. But as Étienne Balibar notes, the question of "What is a Border?" is far more fraught than often recognized. Borders are heterogeneous and ubiquitous and "*some borders are no longer situated at the borders at all*" (Balibar 2002: 84).[5] Borders are territorial, political, juridical, economic, and social (Nail 2016). They include checkpoints, customs offices, and detention centers, as well as private property regimes enforced by police or private security guards. Many borders are diffused through societies with police forces detaining migrants who are unable to establish their legal status. Private actors often assist in maintaining borders: states co-opt airlines, schools, landlords, hotels, and others into verifying immigration status. Other borders are mobile, including checkpoints that extend far into the national territory and roving maritime forces that intercept migrants in international waters.

Importantly, borders do not always restrict mobility; they also facilitate it—as Chris Rumford puts it, "the border can be reconfigured as a portal" (Johnson et al. 2011: 67). For example, airports, train stations, and ports serve to both facilitate and restrict movement for some. Mobility itself also creates and defines borders. Squatters establish neighborhoods, their feet pounding paths across the outskirts of cities. Migrants chart routes to escape surveillance and share them on online networks, attracting still more migrants. Borders and people who move along or across them shape and constitute each other.

Borders studies has also revealed the many ways in which borders are productive. Instead of seeing borders as part of an invisible backdrop that marks off space, borders actively shape social and economic relationships and create identities. In a discussion of Renaissance philosophy and cartography, Sandro Mazzadra and Brett Neilson write about how "borders are involved in making or creating worlds—their role in the scene of *fabrica mundi* ..." (2013: 30). Drawing lines on a map can be a major part of creating a country as these lines come to define the scope of an administration, economy, and citizenry.

Borders also produce categories of people and shape their identities. Migrants within state borders find themselves classified as guests, temporary workers, refugees, foreign students, or "illegals," in ways that structure their lives and determine their options. The productive role of borders goes beyond establishing political communities and migrant status. As Mezzadra and Neilson put it, "borders, far from serving simply to block or obstruct global flows, have become essential devices for their articulation"

(Mezzadra and Neilson 2013: 3). They allow us to contain, classify, and in important respects make the world.

This is possible in part due to what Balibar calls the *"polysemic nature of borders"*—"the fact that they do not have the same meaning for everyone" (Balibar 2002: 81). He illustrates how borders are often invisible to people with privileged citizenships:

> For a rich person from a rich country, a person who tends towards the cosmopolitan (and whose passport increasingly *signifies* not just mere national belonging, protection and a right of citizenship, but a *surplus* of rights—in particular, a world right to circulate unhindered), the border has become an embarkation formality, a point of symbolic acknowledgement of his social status, to be passed at a jog-trot. For a poor person from a poor country, however, the border tends to be something quite different: not only is it an obstacle which is very difficult to surmount, but it is a place he runs up against repeatedly, passing and repassing through it as and when he is expelled or allowed to rejoin his family, so that it becomes, in the end, a place where he *resides*. It is an extraordinarily viscous spatio-temporal zone, almost a home—a home in which to live a life which is a waiting-to-live, a non-life. (Balibar 2002: 83)

Borders are never entirely open or closed—the openness or closure of a border depends on the laws, practices, and techniques that regulate movement and the characteristics of the person trying to move. For this reason, seeing borders in terms of a simple inside/outside dichotomy is a mistake. As Mezzadra and Neilson note, "borders are equally devices of inclusion that select and filter people and different forms of circulation in ways no less violent than those deployed in exclusionary measures" (2013: 7).

Furthermore, borders are not only created by states. Chris Rumford has written extensively on how citizens, entrepreneurs, corporations, NGOs, towns, and others have manipulated and established borders to their advantage:

> The value of asking the question of "who borders?", aside from the obvious benefit of causing us to reconsider one of the "givens" of border studies, is that it brings into view a whole range of borders, not hitherto considered as "real" borders. In doing so it shifts the study of borders from an almost exclusive focus on the state to the broader terrain of society wherein citizens are in fact involved in constructing and contesting borders: creating borders which facilitate mobility for some, while creating barriers to mobility for

others; creating zones which can determine what types of economic activity can be conducted where; contesting the legitimacy of or undermining the borders imposed by others. (Rumford 2006: 23)

This draws attention to the many ways in which people sustain borders through their everyday decisions. The reality of borders depends on people acknowledging them—a border that no one recognizes is not a border at all. By acquiescing to borders, people also confirm their legitimacy. Contrarily, the refusal of borders—by migrants who travel clandestinely or by public protests—can weaken or even abolish them.

Borders can be used to make claims. For example, Dreamers who were brought to the United States as children use their social membership and long-term residence on the territory to claim a legal right to full membership. In doing so, they seek to reconfigure a border. In 2011, 300 young migrant workers in Greece succeeded through a hunger strike in pressuring the Greek government to extend their permission to stay and in some cases to allow them to apply for permanent residence (King 2016; Kuebler 2011).

Conclusion

Methodological nationalism privileges a vision of borders and of space that does not reflect the world. Borders are everywhere, not only at the edges of state territory. In many cases, spaces are transnational. In many more cases, the most significant borders are local, but with local spaces connected to distant territories.

Once we recognize the bias of methodological nationalism, the first step to overcoming it is to find ways of describing the world not dictated by the exigencies of the nation-state. The argument of this chapter is that attempts at inaugurating a cosmopolitan social science, along with research on mobility, transnationalism, and the nature of borders, have laid the groundwork for a more adequate social science.

The task of the next chapter is to explore the implications of this research. What we know about the world and the categories that we use to understand has consequences for what we should do and what sorts of institutions we should endorse. Political philosophy that limits itself to a vision that identifies borders with state borders is impoverished and inadequate. A richer account of borders and a more perspicuous account of migration have much to offer normative theory. In particular, it offers suggestions for how we should frame migration as an issue and about the agents and sites relevant to an account of migration and justice.

Notes

1. As I discuss in the next chapter, corporations and private property holders continue to exercise enormous power over people's movement, in many cases expelling people from land enclosed closed off for development, homes (e.g., during the sub-prime housing crisis), or neighborhoods (e.g., shuffling people without housing into the least desirable areas of the city where they can be ignored). In many cases, private individuals hold others captive through contract and labor law (this is true of much temporary and domestic labor around the world which in some cases becomes a form of slavery) (McCarthy 2014). These private entities derive their authority from the state that enforces exclusions, expulsions, and evictions with police and sometimes soldiers. Even though private actors lack the ultimate authority to police movement, they continue to exercise extraordinary power.
2. Here Beck echoes for Michael Billig's (1995) phrase "banal nationalism."
3. https://www.passportindex.org/byRank.php
4. I use "border" and "boundary" interchangeably. Some scholars distinguish between borders and boundaries, for example, confining "border" to political borders and seeing boundaries as symbolic and social frontiers. However, there is no consistent distinction between the two across disciplines. Moreover, I believe a firm distinction between the two obscures the ways in which political, social, economic, and symbolic processes interact to establish borders (or boundaries). Insisting on a sharp distinction oversimplifies and in some cases misleads us about the nature of borders/boundaries.
5. Italics in original.

References

Agnew, John. 1994. The Territorial Trap: The Geographical Assumptions of International Relations Theory. *Review of International Political Economy* 1 (1): 53–80.

Balibar, Étienne. 2002. *Politics and the Other Scene*. London: Verso.

Bauböck, Rainer, and Thomas Faist, eds. 2010. *A Global Perspective on Transnational Migration: Theorizing Migration Without Methodological Nationalism*. Amsterdam: Amsterdam University Press.

Beck, Ulrich. 2004. Cosmopolitical Realism: On the Distinction Between Cosmopolitanism in Philosophy and the Social Sciences. *Global Networks* 4 (1): 131–156.

Billig, Michael. 1995. *Banal Nationalism*. London, UK: Sage Publications.

Boli, John, and George M. Thomas. 1997. World Culture in the World Polity: A Century of International Non-Governmental Organization. *American Sociological Review* 62 (2): 171–190.

Brown, Wendy. 2010. *Walled States, Waning Sovereignty*. New York and Cambridge, MA: Zone Books and Distributed by the MIT Press.
Castles, Stephen. 2007. Twenty-First-Century Migration as a Challenge to Sociology. *Journal of Ethnic and Migration Studies* 33 (3): 351–371.
Cohen, Elizabeth F. 2009. *Semi-Citizenship in Democratic Politics*. Cambridge and New York: Cambridge University Press.
Collyer, Michael, and Russell King. 2015. Producing Transnational Space: International Migration and the Extra-Territorial Reach of State Power. *Progress in Human Geography* 39 (2): 185–204.
Connolly, William E. 1993. *The Terms of Political Discourse*. 3rd ed. Princeton Paperbacks. Princeton, NJ: Princeton University Press.
Delanty, Gerard. 2009. *The Cosmopolitan Imagination: The Renewal of Critical Social Theory*. Cambridge, UK and New York: Cambridge University Press.
———. 2012. The Idea of Critical Cosmopolitanism. In *Routledge Handbook of Cosmopolitanism Studies*, ed. Gerard Delanty, 38–46. Routledge International Handbooks. Abingdon, Oxon and New York: Routledge.
Deleuze, Gilles, and Félix Guattari. 1987. *A Thousand Plateaus: Capitalism and Schizophrenia*. Minneapolis: University of Minnesota Press.
Ellis, Andrew, Alan Wall, International Institute for Democracy and Electoral Assistance and Instituto Federal Electoral (Mexico), eds. 2007. *Voting from Abroad: The International IDEA Handbook*. Handbook Series. Stockholm, Sweden and Mexico City, Mexico: International IDEA; Federal Electoral Institute of Mexico.
Faist, Thomas, and Jürgen Gerdes. 2008. *Dual Citizenship in the Age of Mobility*. Washington, DC: Migration Policy Institute. http://www.migrationpolicy.org/research/dual-citizenship-age-mobility.
Fassin, Didier. 2011. Policing Borders, Producing Boundaries. The Governmentality of Immigration in Dark Times. *Annual Review of Anthropology* 40 (1): 213–226.
Friedman, Thomas L. 2005. *The World Is Flat: A Brief History of the Twenty-First Century*. New York: Farrar, Straus and Giroux.
Gabaccia, Donna R. 1999. Is Everywhere Nowhere? Nomads, Nations, and the Immigrant Paradigm of United States History. *The Journal of American History* 86 (3): 1115.
Gabaccia, Donna R., and Fraser M. Ottanelli. 2005. *Italian Workers of the World: Labor Migration and the Formation of Multiethnic States*. Urbana, IL: University of Illinois Press.
Gallie, W.B.1955. Essentially Contested Concepts. *Proceedings of the Aristotelian Society*, New Series, 56: 167–198.
Glick Schiller, Nina, Linda Basch, and Cristina Szanton Blanc. 1995. From Immigrant to Transmigrant: Theorizing Transnational Migration. *Anthropological Quarterly* 68 (1): 46–63.

Harvey, David. 1989. *The Condition of Postmodernity*. Cambridge, MA: Basil Blackwell.
Held, David. 1995. *Democracy and the Global Order: From the Modern State to Cosmopolitan Governance*. Stanford, CA: Stanford University Press.
———. 1999. The Transformation of Political Community: Rethinking Democracy in the Context of Globalization. In *Democracy's Edges*, ed. Ian Shapiro and Casiano Hacker-Cordón, 84–111. Contemporary Political Theory. London and New York: Cambridge University Press.
Johnson, Corey, Reece Jones, Anssi Paasi, Louise Amoore, Alison Mountz, Mark Salter, and Chris Rumford. 2011. Interventions on Rethinking 'the Border' in Border Studies. *Political Geography* 30 (2): 61–69.
Jones, Reece. 2016. Borders and Walls: Do Barriers Deter Unauthorized Migration? Migration Policy Institute. http://www.migrationpolicy.org/article/borders-and-walls-do-barriers-deter-unauthorized-migration
Keohane, Robert O., and Joseph S. Nye. 1972. *Transnational Relations and World Politics*. Cambridge, MA: Harvard University Press.
King, Natasha. 2016. *No Borders: The Politics of Immigration Control and Resistance*. London: Zed Books.
Krasner, Stephen D. 1999. *Sovereignty: Organized Hypocrisy*. Princeton, NJ: Princeton University Press.
Kuebler, Martin. 2011. Greek Migrants End Hunger Strike. *Deutsche Welle*, October 3. http://www.dw.com/en/greek-migrants-end-hunger-strike/a-14902489
Levitt, Peggy, and B. Nadya Jaworsky. 2007. Transnational Migration Studies: Past Developments and Future Trends. *Annual Review of Sociology* 33 (1): 129–156.
Malešević, Siniša. 2017. Empires and Nation-States: Beyond the Dichotomy. *Thesis Eleven* 139 (1): 3–10.
Massey, Douglas S., Jorge Durand, and Karen A. Pren. 2016. Why Border Enforcement Backfired. *American Journal of Sociology* 121 (5): 1557–1600.
McCarthy, Lauren A. 2014. Human Trafficking and the New Slavery. *Annual Review of Law and Social Science* 10 (1): 221–242.
Meyer, John W., John Boli, George M. Thomas, and Francisco O. Ramirez. 1997. World Society and the Nation-State. *American Journal of Sociology* 103 (1): 144–181.
Mezzadra, Sandro, and Brett Neilson. 2013. *Border as Method, or, the Multiplication of Labor*. Durham: Duke University Press.
Miller, David. 2016. *Strangers in Our Midst: The Political Philosophy of Immigration*. Cambridge, MA: Harvard University Press.
Nail, Thomas. 2015. *The Figure of the Migrant*. Stanford, CA: Stanford University Press.

———. 2016. *Theory of the Border.* Oxford and New York: Oxford University Press.
Nussbaum, Martha Craven. 2007. *Frontiers of Justice: Disability, Nationality, Species Membership.* The Tanner Lectures on Human Values. Cambridge, MA: Belknap Press of Harvard University Press.
Papadopoulos, Dimitris, and Vassilis S. Tsianos. 2013. After Citizenship: Autonomy of Migration, Organisational Ontology and Mobile Commons. *Citizenship Studies* 17 (2): 178–196.
Ringmar, Erik. Forthcoming. The Anti-Nomadic Bias of Political Theory. In *Nomad-State Relationships in International Relations: Before and After Borders*, ed. Jamie Levin. Basingstoke: Palgrave.
Rumford, C. 2006. Theorizing Borders. *European Journal of Social Theory* 9 (2): 155–169.
Rumford, Chris. 2014a. 'Seeing Like a Border': Towards Multiperspectivalism. In *Cosmopolitan Borders*, ed. Chris Rumford, 39–54. London: Palgrave Macmillan UK.
———. 2014b. *Cosmopolitan Borders.* Houndmills, Basingstoke, Hampshire and New York, NY: Palgrave Macmillan.
Salazar, Noel B. 2017. Key Figures of Mobility: An Introduction: Key Figures of Mobility. *Social Anthropology* 25 (1): 5–12.
Sassen, Saskia. 2014. *Expulsions: Brutality and Complexity in the Global Economy.* Cambridge, MA: The Belknap Press of Harvard University Press.
Scott, James C. 2009. *The Art of Not Being Governed: An Anarchist History of Upland Southeast Asia.* Yale Agrarian Studies Series. New Haven: Yale University Press.
Scott, James C. 2017. *Against the Grain: A Deep History of the Earliest States.* Yale Agrarian Studies. New Haven: Yale University Press.
Sheller, Mimi, and John Urry. 2006. The New Mobilities Paradigm. *Environment and Planning A* 38 (2): 207–226.
Slaughter, Anne-Marie. 2005. *A New World Order.* Princeton, NJ: Princeton University Press.
Stark, Oded. 1991. *The Migration of Labor.* Cambridge, MA and Oxford, UK: B. Blackwell.
Torpey, John. 1998. Coming and Going: On the State Monopolization of the Legitimate 'Means of Movement'. *Sociological Theory* 16 (3): 239–259.
Urry, John. 2007. *Mobilities.* Malden, MA: Polity.
Vallet, Élisabeth, and Charles-Philippe David. 2012. Introduction: The (Re)Building of the Wall in International Relations. *Journal of Borderlands Studies* 27 (2): 111–119.
Young, Iris Marion. 2011. *Justice and the Politics of Difference.* Paperback reissue. Princeton, NJ: Princeton University Press.

CHAPTER 4

Sites, Systems, and Agents

Abstract This chapter continues the task of enriching the categories and considerations for an ethics of mobility. It insists that determining causality is central to identifying moral responsibility. It urges locating migration within broader trends of often inequitable social transformation. This requires attention to global political economy, as well as to migration systems which bind people and regions together through historical, economic, cultural, and political relationships. It also advocates for more moral scrutiny of corporate actors and for greater attention to internal migration and mobility restrictions within cities.

Keywords Mobility • Corporations • Political economy • Migration systems • Cities

The previous chapter provided an overview of research projects that allow us to study migration without the blinders of methodological nationalism. In this chapter, I want to explore how this research gives rise to new questions and draws attention to alternative sites and agents relevant to normative thinking about borders and mobility. Abjuring methodological nationalism does not mean eliminating the nation-state from our analysis. It does, however, provide grounds for rejecting accounts that see the nation-state as defining the site and scope of justice. The literature on cosmopolitan social science, mobility, transnationalism, and borders

© The Author(s) 2018
A. Sager, *Toward a Cosmopolitan Ethics of Mobility*,
Mobility & Politics, https://doi.org/10.1007/978-3-319-65759-2_4

reveals that the dichotomy between global and national is untenable. The nation-state is one agent and one site among many others embedded in complex migration systems.

Normative theorists should situate their inquiries within global political economy and broad processes of social and economic transformation. Attention to these processes leads us to migration systems sustained by a migration industry and policies that cut across states and regions. It also encourages us to explore internal migration, especially from rural to urban areas within states. Finally, cities are major actors within migration systems, as well as sites that raise their own moral issues about mobility. In particular, we should turn our attention to how mobility is regulated in many of the world's metropolises through segregation by race, ethnicity, nationality, and class.

GLOBAL POLITICAL ECONOMY AND MIGRATION SYSTEMS

Causality is fundamental to normative theory. When we wish to assign moral responsibility, we need to be able to identify agents responsible for wrongdoing. Moreover, we need to explain what they did, why they did it, and how they did it. "How" questions also involve understanding how institutions structure outcomes. These include laws and bureaucracies, but also widespread social norms and attitudes that can undergird systemic or institutional discrimination (e.g., racism or sexism). Though responsibility is often indirect and diffusely shared, people nonetheless have responsibilities to reform, abolish, and replace unjust institutions.

Determining causality is an enormously challenging task in any area, but migration is particularly fraught with multiple, possibly competing, possibly complementary theories in play (Massey et al. 1998; Haas 2010). Furthermore, disciplinary boundaries encourage us to analyze migration in isolation, obscuring how migration is a component of other economic, social, and political processes (Brettell and Hollifield 2008). These processes cause migration which in turn shapes the economic, social, political, and physical environment. Stephen Castles writes:

> An alternative approach is to conceptualize migration not merely as a result of social transformation, nor as one of its causes, but as an integral and essential part of social transformation processes. That means that theories of migration should be embedded in broader social theory. It also means that research on any specific migration phenomenon must always include

research on the societal context in which it takes place. Finally, because awareness of change starts usually at the local level, it is important to link local-level experiences of migration (whether in origin or receiving areas) with other socio-spatial levels—and particularly with global processes. (Castles 2010: 1578)

If we follow Castle's recommendation and conceptualize migration as an essential part of social transformation, then the broadest level of analysis will be global. Though they have fallen out of favor in many circles, approaches to migration that take a historical-structural approach and draw on Marxism, dependency theory, and world-systems theory continue to provide valuable insights (Massey et al. 1998: 34–41). International migration is a result of the global economy incorporating peripheral regions, establishing links, and uprooting populations. Migration occurs in a context of extraordinary social change that has transformed people's lives and livelihoods. These changes need to be situated in their historical context (including colonial relationships) and must take into account foreign investment, the creation of labor markets, resource extraction, and military links.

Again, Castles usefully summarizes some of these developments:

At a structural level, social transformation in developed countries can be seen in the closure of older industries, the restructuring of labor forces, the erosion of welfare states, the fragmentation of communities and the reshaping of social identities. In less-developed countries, forms of social transformation include intensification of agriculture, destruction of rural livelihoods, erosion of local social orders, and the formation of shanty-towns within new mega-cities. (Castles 2010: 1576)

Saskia Sassen has written extensively on how foreign investment structures migration. It leads to internal migration as people move from rural to urban settings and from agricultural-based subsistence living to wage labor. Rural to urban migration sets the stage for international migration as Export Processing Zones directly link regions (Sassen 1988: 12–25). Developed countries and their proxies such as multinational corporations not only invest. They also demand low-wage workers for jobs in segmented labor markets that attract workers from abroad (Piore 1979). Nowhere is this starker than in global cities where migrants labor to provide services and care for global elites (Sassen 2008).

These social transformations are rarely equitable. Even when they bring benefits, they often have devastating consequences for the most vulnerable members of the society. They often involve what David Harvey (2005) has described as "accumulation through dispossession" through a variety of legal and political mechanisms, including land consolidation, commodifying labor and natural resources, environmental degradation, financial speculation, and privatization of the commons. Dispossession has been a major consequence of neoliberal privatization and the defunding of the public sector, often under the mandate and guidance of international organizations (Stiglitz 2003). Mobility often becomes a survival strategy in these circumstances. This has the effect of blurring the line between voluntary and involuntary migration where many people ostensibly moving for economic motivations are in fact better described as fleeing destitution.[1]

Normative theorists need to reflect on how migration occurs in these contexts. Too often they assume that migration is simply a result of poverty and strife that creates a "push" factor and the wealth and opportunities "pulling" migrants to wealthier regions. Nationalist political philosophers express regret that foreign nations have failed to ensure the prosperity of their citizens, but are indignant that strangers might think they have a right to immigrate to the "developed" world (Miller 2007). This ignores how migration is never simply a matter of "pushes" and "pulls." Simply knowing that people are poor tells us little about whether they will migrate and even less about where they might travel. Focusing on the global economy—and on the ways in which powerful states and actors have shaped it—allows us to connect capital flows with labor flows and structural processes. This also helps us to assign moral responsibility; if we can determine which actors caused people to move under adverse circumstances, we can begin to outline obligations to mitigate harm.

Global political trends and processes are not sufficiently fine-grained for assigning responsibility. Nonetheless, macro-economic analysis immediately suggests units of analysis other than the nation-state. Of particular importance are migration systems (Kritz et al. 1992). The first generation of migrants often arrive through corporate or state recruitment (e.g., through guest worker programs). Though migration flows may begin with formal, institutional efforts to attract workers, migrants maintain connections with the families and communities abroad. This gives rise to informal networks, connecting people by providing information about opportunities and resources that enable others to travel. Social networks provide social capital that reduces the costs and risks of migrating. In many countries, family reunification policies facilitate chain migration, further strengthening networks. These networks sustain transnational communities with migrants actively involved in politics and economic development across borders. When cross-border networks give rise to an extensive migration industry that supports migration, they become migration systems. Migration systems link regions economically and politically.[2]

Attention to migration systems alerts us to many neglected actors that shape migration flows and incur moral responsibilities. Too often moral theorists see migration in terms of the relationship between individual migrants and the state or community, ignoring the other parties involved in facilitating movement. One neglected actor is the corporation, which has a major and direct influence on migration flows. Matthew Frye Jacobson observes:

> The corporate story behind immigration history—the dance of these elephants, their labor practices and the regional impact of their conduct, their increasing mobility and the trend toward the increased internationalization of production, the migrants they lure and also the residents they displace—here is a story that we have not yet begun to come to grips with. (2006: 83)

These include corporations seeking workers, recruiters, travel agents, and development agencies. Businesses employ migrants and lobby for immigration policies that favor their industries. They secure visas for some employees and knowingly employ others without the legal authority to work in the country. In many countries, entire industries are structurally dependent on migrant labor.

Businesses not only employ and rely on migrants. They are also major players in the migration industry, profiting by providing a range of services that facilitate and hinder movement. They serve as intermediaries that recruit migrants (Martin 2005). In many cases, they extend loans, facilitating movement, while delivering workers into the hands of exploitative and abusive employers on whom they must depend if they are to have any hope of paying their debts. In the worst cases, this becomes indentured labor or modern-day slavery (McCarthy 2014). Private corporations also respond to the outsourcing of border controls. This in turn contributes to the black market for smugglers to facilitate travel once licit routes are closed (Sanchez 2015).

Corporations' power to significantly shape migration policy comes with corresponding responsibilities. They have duties to provide their workers with safe working conditions and fair salaries. They also have obligations to the communities where they are located. If state migration policies are unjust, corporations that provide surveillance systems, private prisons, or barbed wire abet injustice.

Corporations form only part of the migration industry (Andersson 2014). Humanitarian organizations also react to refugee flows and the human misery caused by increased border controls—as well as fill gaps in assistance where the state has abdicated its responsibilities. In many cases, they become implicated in migration enforcement with humanitarianism simultaneously serving surveillance and control even as its agents provide aid. Migrant rights and civil society groups attempt to shape policy and public discourse, as well as support them in their travels and struggles with state legal systems. Groups opposing immigration campaign to reduce quotas and increase penalties for those moving without authorization, as well as for people who help them. Churches mobilize their congregations and extend sanctuary. Journalists and academics shape discourse as they pursue their careers, raising ethical questions about research and representation.

Migration systems have important implications for normative accounts of distributive justice that attempt to restrict justice's scope. In particular, they destabilize debates that pit cosmopolitans against statists and nationalists. At the risk of oversimplification, cosmopolitan accounts of global justice take individuals as the fundamental unit of moral concern. If groups have moral value, it ultimately derives from the value they have for their individual members. Furthermore, people matter equally for cosmopolitans, regardless of their sex, gender, ethnic group, race, nationality, or class. Finally—and most controversially—moral concern applies globally: our moral obligations are to humanity. In determining what we ought to do, it is unjust to give special weight to our fellow citizens or community members *simply because* they are our fellow citizens or community members (Nussbaum 2002; Pogge 2002). There may be practical reasons to favor people within our community (e.g., we may be better situated to help), but the mere fact that they are part of our community provides no moral weight.

Nationalist and statist objections to cosmopolitan accounts of justice attempt to identify a feature of nation-states that provided grounds for privileging compatriots. In most cases, this involves showing how different types of associations ground special claims. Nationalists seek to show

how national identities and shared values give people reasons for privileging their compatriots (Kymlicka 2015; Miller 2007). Statists insist that justice should be located within the state, in some cases citing the need to justify coercively imposed institutions to people under their power (Blake 2001; Nagel 2005). Other statists credit the role of reciprocal relationships between citizens in providing collective goods as giving rise to special moral claims (Sangiovanni 2007). Debates between cosmopolitans, nationalists, and statists oscillate around the extent to which associations and institutions across borders support an account of global justice. Nationalists and statists hold that the relationships and institutions at the level of the nation-state are special: our connections to members of our territorial-based national community are different in kind from the connections we have to outsiders. Cosmopolitans respond by attempting to show the extent of coercion and cooperation at the international and global level (Abizadeh 2007).

Much of this debate has remained within the grips of methodological nationalism. Nationalist and statist accounts define the nation-state as their unit of analysis, taking territorial borders for granted and identifying state with society. This could hardly be otherwise, but cosmopolitan accounts also tend to adopt methodological nationalist assumptions. For example, obligations of global justice are often seen in terms of *state* obligations to give foreign development aid, permit immigration, or otherwise redistribute resources. Cosmopolitans—including those working on migration—remain far too sanguine that global justice could be achieved in a world where nation-states are the major actors.[3]

This vision of global justice becomes untenable once we break free of methodological nationalism. Migration systems reveal the extent that migration is a result of deliberate political and economic decisions bringing people together across state borders in webs of cooperation. These decisions are often largely independent of state-level actors, and even when they take the form of laws or bureaucratic procedures, private actors often play a decisive role in shaping them. Moreover, many associations are transcultural, disrupting simplistic nationalist narratives that seek to obliterate cross-border connections. Finally, these migration systems are maintained by coercion, including border control regimes that admit some, allow others to settle, and employ considerable violence in the effort to exclude others.

For example, the United States and Mexico or France and Northern Africa—to mention two prominent migration systems—are closely bound by historical, economic, cultural, and political relationships (Delgado Wise and Márquez Covarrubias 2008; Haas 2008). These relationships have largely been asymmetrical, with the United States and France exercising unequal power over their counterparts. Nonetheless, the deep institutional bonds between the regions suggest seeing migration not as a matter of moving from one country to another, but rather as traversing a dense set of links that bring individuals and communities together. To pretend that the United States or France can morally extricate itself from their deep, long-standing connections that have supported migration for decades (or in the case of the United States centuries) is disingenuous. An adequate moral theory cannot treat states as isolated "containers." Rather, it must examine the deep connections that bind regions and people together and affect their well-being and fate.

CITIES AND THE NATIONAL RURAL-URBAN DIVIDE

Methodological nationalism also blinds us to diversity within societies (and to transnational connections that contribute to this diversity). Debates about global justice mired in methodological nationalism lead us to frame the debate in terms of the obligations of rich states to poor states, overlooking the pockets of affluence surrounded by penury and the dire poverty within many of the world's wealthiest states. Ethical questions concerning international migration have mostly been analyzed independently of ethical questions about mobility within state territories. This is puzzling, since mobility within states has many of the same causes (e.g., relocation for better opportunities, structural transformation of the economy and the physical environment, persecution and violence). Mobility restrictions within states also raise many of the same ethical issues about freedom of movement, access to opportunities, cultural and environmental change, and unjust discrimination.

Most people treat global and national justice as empirically and conceptually separate. Mobility restrictions across borders are recognized as potentially subject to moral scrutiny, whereas normative theorists, especially within political philosophy, mostly ignore mobility at the domestic level.[4] This leads to a moral distinction between the exclusion of foreigners from national territories and the exclusion of citizens within territories. There is a broad consensus that *de jure* segregation within the nation is unambiguously unjust, whereas legal prohibitions on immigration are legitimate.

In fact these two issues are closely connected. The influence of methodological nationalism in the social sciences and in our normative theorizing has led us to ignore the similarities between forms of exclusion, as well as to neglect their interactions. It helps explain why the ethics of international and internal mobility have mostly been analyzed separately. Methodological nationalists who see migration controls primarily as a question of entry at state borders overlook the many ways in which social boundaries exclude people present on the territory in equally morally problematic ways (Bertram 2014). Many of the ethical issues in international migration deserve to be connected to the literature on segregation, gentrification, and the privatization of public space. Since these issues affect not only long-term residents, but also many recent migrants, attention to internal mobility not only complements an analysis of international mobility, but also completes it.

As discussed above, the nation-state frame blinds us to structural changes in the global economy that have transformed regional job markets. The boundaries between internal and international mobility are often vague and in many cases both types of migrants respond to the same sorts of causes (King and Skeldon 2010). In many parts of the world, rural populations can no longer sustain themselves and must migrate to urban centers. In many places, rural areas—including within rich states—have trouble attracting health care and other professionals who prefer urban living. These shortages parallel situations that have led to prominent cries against international "brain drain," but receive little moral scrutiny (Sager 2014).

By classifying migration as international migration, we also overlook questions about distributive justice and unjust labor discrimination. Discussions of immigration and equality often take place exclusively at the level of countries: a move from a lower wage region to a higher wage region is seen as a straightforward gain. The reality is more fine-grained. Immigrants may be subject to deskilling or "brain waste" (the underemployment of skilled professional migrants), so that even if they benefit economically in comparison to their situation before immigrating, they may be unjustly disadvantaged in their new country. When asking questions about distributive justice, we need to think carefully about the scope we assign to our questions: a distribution that appears just at one level (e.g., within the nation-state) may be unacceptable once we broaden or narrow who is included.

The strong parallels between international mobility controls and domestic practices challenge attempts to analyze their morality separately. Thomas Nail usefully connects contemporary immigration law in the United States and the United Kingdom with anti-vagabond legislation of previous centuries (Nail 2015: 206–209). He observes that "vagrancy" laws have been "replaced with a host of related anti-migrant laws against 'loitering,' 'riotous activities,' 'the obstruction of streets and sidewalks,' 'camping,' 'sitting/lying in public places,' 'panhandling,' and 'begging'" (Nail 2015: 208).[5] These practices of course continue and combine with laws designed to detain, deport, and segregate international migrants.

In some cases, such as with the Chinese *hukou* system, mobility controls segregate rural and urban populations, illegalizing rural workers who leave the countryside for the city (Chan 2010). Chandran Kukathas (2015) and Jonathan Moses (2006) have drawn provocative analogies between immigration controls and South African apartheid, noting how immigration controls are largely aimed at controlling specific groups' behavior within the territory: how long they can stay, if and where they can work and study, and what services they can access. These controls are backed by state coercion and a violent deportation regime (De Genova and Peutz 2010). Moses connects apartheid and the international migration system. We now condemn South Africa's internal passports and permit systems that black South Africans were forced to endure if they needed to travel or to take or change a job, while seeing rigid controls at international borders as natural and justified. This leads Moses to ask, "Why is the Dane's advantage over the Somalian legitimate (and protected by international law), while the Afrikaner's advantage over the Xosi was not?" (Moses 2006: 85).

Nowhere are these mobility restrictions more striking than in the world's cities where space and architecture shape public life, contribute to the creation of unequal citizenship, and undermine democratic politics (Bickford 2000). Gated communities and suburbs preserve privilege; other populations are regulated to ghettos (Duneier 2016; Low 2004). Financial elites live in lofts or visit hotels in the centers of power, while service staff run the public transportation gauntlet to the low-wage jobs that make possible financial capitalism's opulence. People's mobility—and therefore their opportunities—is shaped by market forces that segregate by income and social class and by the privatization of formerly public space (Harvey 2013). More insidiously, access to public transportation prevents large segments of the population from visiting or working in many neighborhoods. Racism combines with law enforcement where some groups receive special scrutiny, effectively barring them from parts of the city if they do not wish to have their presence challenged.

Cities are sites where groups experience stark differences in rights, opportunities, and status, possessing degrees of what Elizabeth Cohen calls "semi-citizenship":

> As long as we privilege immigration in discussions of anomalies of citizenship, and simultaneously fail to recognize the ways in which semi-citizenships—both those arising from immigration and from other forms of difference—are not new but nearly omnipresent in the politics of states and state-like organizations, we cannot fully or effectively theorize their shapes, causes, or the ways in which they might be governed. (Cohen 2009: 53–54)

Notably, these exclusions affect migrants and long-term residents alike. The inequality and disadvantage suffered by many African-Americans today have their roots in discriminatory housing practices imposed when many migrated to the North of the United States (Massey 2007). International migrants too are often subjected to discrimination and spatial segregation that disadvantage them and limit their opportunities.

Attention to cities offers new trajectories for well-trodden paths in the ethics of migration. For example, political theorists follow politicians in the media in framing ethnic "ghettos" in terms of a failure of immigrants to integrate (or only slightly more generously, a failure on the part of the majority to facilitate their integration). This overlooks how ethnic neighborhoods are often a result of mobility restrictions.

We also need to explore in more detail the connections between the exclusion and inclusion of immigrants from abroad and the internal forms of exclusion and inclusion that affect immigrants (along with many others). As should be evident from the debates in the United States around "sanctuary cities," cities have extensive resources that can shield immigrants from state enforcement or facilitate detention and deportation. External exclusion enables and reinforces internal exclusion within the territory, allowing political entrepreneurs to pretend that parts of the population do not belong. The category of "immigrant" combines with categories of race, gender, and class to reinforce asymmetrical power relations and opportunity hoarding. Expressions such as *français de souche*, *gastarbeiter*, or "real Americans" assume a hierarchy of belonging. Labeling people as foreign— as "aliens" or "illegals"—makes it easier to demonize and scapegoat them, creating an "Us versus Them" dynamic (Anderson 2013; Santa Ana 2002).

Conclusion

In the last two chapters, I have advocated for a wider set of sites and agendas relevant to an ethics of mobility and of borders. Mostly, I have focused on contributions from the social sciences that help us understand the world, as well as suggested how these contributions may be relevant for normative theory. I argued in Chap. 2 that political philosophy is in fact in the grips of methodological nationalism: political philosophers have largely omitted or distorted many of the salient ethical questions about how we draw boundaries and police mobility. I have not explored in depth what political philosophers have to say positively about mobility and borders. The task of the next chapter is two-fold: to evaluate the political philosopher's positive contributions and to suggest building blocks for a more adequate ethics of borders.

Notes

1. I suggest some of the implications that migration theory brings to distributive justice in Sager (2012a) and offer reflections on how considerations of class, inequality, and economic transformations affect global justice in Sager (2012b).
2. This discussion draws on Goldin et al. (2011: 103–109).
3. For a notable exception, see Hidalgo (2016).
4. An important exception is Young (2011). Imbriosco (2004) cautions against using mobility as a poverty-alleviation strategy at the level of the city. This should serve as a warning against proposals that uncritically see international migration as the solution to world poverty. (In both cases, matters are complex.) Also see Hayward and Swanstrom (2011).
5. Also see the first chapter of Bridget Anderson's *Us and Them?: The Dangerous Politics of Immigration Control* (2013) for discussion of vagrancy laws.

References

Abizadeh, Arash. 2007. Cooperation, Pervasive Impact, and Coercion: On the Scope (Not Site) of Distributive Justice. *Philosophy & Public Affairs* 35 (4): 318–358.

Anderson, Bridget. 2013. *Us and Them?* Oxford, UK: Oxford University Press.

Andersson, Ruben. 2014. *Illegality, Inc.: Clandestine Migration and the Business of Bordering Europe*. California Series in Public Anthropology 28. Oakland, CA: University of California Press.

Bertram, Christopher. 2014. Competing Methods of Territorial Control, Migration and Justice. *Critical Review of International Social and Political Philosophy* 17 (1): 129–143.

Bickford, S. 2000. Constructing Inequality: City Spaces and the Architecture of Citizenship. *Political Theory* 28 (3): 355–376.

Blake, Michael. 2001. Distributive Justice, State Coercion, and Autonomy. *Philosophy & Public Affairs* 30 (3): 257–296.

Brettell, Caroline, and James Frank Hollifield, eds. 2008. *Migration Theory: Talking Across Disciplines*. 2nd ed. New York: Routledge.

Castles, Stephen. 2010. Understanding Global Migration: A Social Transformation Perspective. *Journal of Ethnic and Migration Studies* 36 (10): 1565–1586.

Chan, Kam Wing. 2010. The Household Registration System and Migrant Labor in China: Notes on a Debate. *Population and Development Review* 36 (2): 357–364.

Cohen, Elizabeth F. 2009. *Semi-Citizenship in Democratic Politics*. Cambridge and New York: Cambridge University Press.

De Genova, Nicholas, and Nathalie Mae Peutz, eds. 2010. *The Deportation Regime: Sovereignty, Space, and the Freedom of Movement*. Durham, NC: Duke University Press.

Delgado Wise, Stephen, and Humberto Márquez Covarrubias. 2008. The Mexico-United States Migratory System: Dilemmas of Regional Integration, Development, and Emigration. In *Migration and Development: Perspectives from the South*, ed. Stephen Castles, Raúl Delgado Wise, and International Organization for Migration, 113–142. Geneva: IOM International Organization for Migration.

Duneier, Mitchell. 2016. *Ghetto: The Invention of a Place, the History of an Idea*. 1st ed. New York: Farrar, Straus and Giroux.

Goldin, Ian, Geoffrey Cameron, and Meera Balarajan. 2011. *Exceptional People: How Migration Shaped Our World and Will Define Our Future*. Princeton: Princeton University Press.

de Haas, Hein. 2008. North African Migration Systems: Evolution, Transformations, and Development Linkages. In *Migration and Development: Perspectives from the South*, ed. Stephen Castles, Raúl Delgado Wise, and International Organization for Migration. Geneva: IOM International Organization for Migration.

———. 2010. The Internal Dynamics of Migration Processes: A Theoretical Inquiry. *Journal of Ethnic and Migration Studies* 36 (10): 1587–1617.

Harvey, David. 2005. *The New Imperialism*. Oxford and New York: Oxford University Press.

———. 2013. *Rebel Cities: From the Right to the City to the Urban Revolution*. Paperback ed. London: Verso.

Hayward, Clarissa Rile, and Todd Swanstrom, eds. 2011. *Justice and the American Metropolis*. Globalization and Community, v. 18. Minneapolis: University of Minnesota Press.
Hidalgo, Javier. 2016. The Case for the International Governance of Immigration. *International Theory* 8 (01): 140–170.
Imbroscio, David L. 2004. Fighting Poverty with Mobility: A Normative Policy Analysis. *Review of Policy Research* 21 (3): 447–461.
Jacobson, Matthew Frye. 2006. More 'Trans-,' Less 'National'. *Journal of American Ethnic History* 25 (4): 74–84.
King, Russell, and Ronald Skeldon. 2010. 'Mind the Gap!' Integrating Approaches to Internal and International Migration. *Journal of Ethnic and Migration Studies* 36 (10): 1619–1646.
Kritz, Mary M., Lin Lean Lim, and Hania Zlotnik, eds. 1992. *International Migration Systems: A Global Approach*. International Studies in Demography. Oxford and New York: Clarendon Press and Oxford University Press.
Kukathas, Chandran. 2015. Why Immigration Controls Resemble Apartheid in Their Adverse Consequences for Freedom. *Democratic Audit UK*, September 15. http://www.democraticaudit.com/2015/09/15/why-immigration-controls-resemble-apartheid-in-their-adverse-consequences-for-freedom/
Kymlicka, Will. 2015. Solidarity in Diverse Societies: Beyond Neoliberal Multiculturalism and Welfare Chauvinism. *Comparative Migration Studies* 3 (1): 1–19.
Low, Setha M. 2004. *Behind the Gates: Life, Security, and the Pursuit of Happiness in Fortress America*. New York, NY: Routledge.
Martin, Philip. 2005. *Merchants of Labor: Agents of the Evolving Migration Infrastructure*. Discussion Paper. Geneva: International Institute for Labour Studies 158.
Massey, Douglas S. 2007. *Categorically Unequal: The American Stratification System*. A Russell Sage Foundation Centennial Volume. New York: Russell Sage Foundation.
Massey, Douglas S., Joaquín Arango, Graeme Hugo, Ali Kouaouci, Adela Pellegrino, and J. Edward Taylor, eds. 1998. *Worlds in Motion: Understanding International Migration at the End of the Millennium*. International Studies in Demography. New York: Clarendon Press.
McCarthy, Lauren A. 2014. Human Trafficking and the New Slavery. *Annual Review of Law and Social Science* 10 (1): 221–242.
Miller, David. 2007. *National Responsibility and Global Justice*. Oxford and New York: Oxford University Press.
Moses, Jonathon Wayne. 2006. *International Migration: Globalization's Last Frontier*. Global Issues. New York, NY: Zed Books.
Nagel, Thomas. 2005. The Problem of Global Justice. *Philosophy and Public Affairs* 33 (2): 113–147.

Nail, Thomas. 2015. *The Figure of the Migrant*. Stanford, CA: Stanford University Press.
Nussbaum, Martha Craven. 2002. *For Love of Country?* Edited by Joshua Cohen. New Democracy Forum. Boston: Beacon Press.
Piore, Michael J. 1979. *Birds of Passage: Migrant Labor and Industrial Societies*. Cambridge and New York: Cambridge University Press.
Pogge, Thomas Winfried Menko. 2002. *World Poverty and Human Rights: Cosmopolitan Responsibilities and Reforms*. Cambridge and Malden, MA: Polity.
Sager, Alex. 2012a. The Implications of Migration Theory for Distributive Justice. *Global Justice: Theory, Practice, Rhetoric* 5: 56–70.
———. 2012b. Immigration, Class, and Global Justice: Some Moral Considerations/Implications. In *La Communauté Politique En Question. Regards Croisés Sur L'immigration, La Citoyenneté, La Diversité et Le Pouvoir*, ed. Micheline Labelle, Jocelyne Couture, and Frank Remiggi. Quebec: UQAM Press.
———. 2014. Political Rights, Republican Freedom, and Temporary Workers. *Critical Review of International Social and Political Philosophy* 17 (2): 189–211.
Sanchez, Gabriella E. 2015. *Human Smuggling and Border Crossings*. Routledge Studies in Criminal Justice, Borders and Citizenship. London and New York, NY: Routledge.
Sangiovanni, Andrea. 2007. Global Justice, Reciprocity, and the State. *Philosophy & Public Affairs* 35 (1): 3–39.
Santa Ana, Otto. 2002. *Brown Tide Rising: Metaphors of Latinos in Contemporary American Public Discourse*. Austin: University of Texas Press.
Sassen, Saskia. 1988. *The Mobility of Labor and Capital: A Study in International Investment and Labor Flow*. Cambridge, UK and New York: Cambridge University Press.
———. 2008. Two Stops in Today's New Global Geographies: Shaping Novel Labor Supplies and Employment Regimes. *American Behavioral Scientist* 52 (3): 457–496.
Stiglitz, Joseph E. 2003. *Globalization and Its Discontents*. New York: W.W. Norton.
Young, Iris Marion. 2011. *Justice and the Politics of Difference*. Paperback reissue. Princeton, NJ: Princeton University Press.

CHAPTER 5

Critical Cosmopolitanism and the Ethics of Mobility

Abstract This chapter sets out criteria for a critical cosmopolitan account of the political philosophy of migration. It develops this account through an exploration of Matheiu Kassovitz's film *La Haine* that follows three youth from the *banlieue* of Chateloup-les-Vignes in the aftermath of neighborhood clashes with the police. The multidimensional forms of exclusion that the *banlieue* youth experience suggest the need for a more complex ethics of borders. To guide the search for this ethics, the chapter outlines a critical cosmopolitan ethics of migration and borders that combines insights from the social sciences and philosophy and seeks to promote people's capabilities and to contest relationships of domination and hierarchy.

Keywords Critical cosmopolitanism • Capabilities • Domination • Hierarchy • *La Haine* • Political philosophy

The last two chapters canvassed insights from the social sciences to show how we can think about migration without falling prey to methodological nationalism. In this final chapter, I use the film *La Haine* as an illustration of the complexity of the ethical issues surrounding mobility and borders that arise when we give more attention to the multiple sites in which people's mobility is constrained. This leads to a series of reflections on the ethics of borders. I advocate for the need of activists and social scientists to more closely engage normative work in political philosophy. Similarly, political philosophers should turn to scholarship that offers a richer account of borders. I end by proposing criteria to guide the construction of a more adequate ethics of borders and mobility.

LA HAINE

Mathieu Kassovitz's 1995 *La Haine* (*Hate*) opens with archival footage of protests in response to police brutality. In 1995, Officer Pascal Compain placed his pistol against the head of 17-year-old Makomé M'Bowolé, allegedly to frighten him into confessing. But instead of obtaining a confession, Compain's pistol went off, killing M'Bowolé.[1] The footage shows riot police covering van windows with metal grills, protestors marching, and youth burning cars. Bob Marley's "Lootin' and Burnin'" plays. Police in riot gear lob tear gas and beat and arrest those who fall. In the background, graffiti reads, "Que justice soit faite pour Mako"—that justice be done for Mako.

Fiction sometimes captures the *zeitgeist* more effectively than the headlines. *La Haine* follows three young men from the *banlieue*[2] of Chanteloup-les-Vignes—Vinz (Jewish), Hubert (black African), and Saïd (Arab)—in the wake of the clashes with police that left their friend Abdel Ichaha in a coma. Though the film is loosely structured around Vinz's discovery of a policeman's .44 Magnum and his vow to take revenge if their friend Abdel dies, what holds the film together is not the plot, but rather the aggressive comradery of the trio against the architecture and city blocks captured by the black and white cinematography. *La Haine* is a film about the alienation and the *banlieue* youth's hatred of the police, a hatred that is in many respects reciprocated. It is also is a film about place, about exclusion, and about borders and boundaries.

The Chanteloup-les-Vignes (at least as depicted in the film) is an occupied territory. Youth are constantly subject to police surveillance and harassment. Police arrive to expel neighbors who have gathered to roast hotdogs and escape the heat. Though youth from the *banlieue* are spatially and socially excluded, they are also banally cosmopolitan. Hubert, Saïd, and Vinz causally allude to Lethal Weapon, Taxi Driver, and MacGyver. A DJ in a Cypress Hill t-shirt places a speaker in his high-rise window and blasts a mix of N.W.A.'s "Fuck the Police" and Edith Piaf's *Je ne regretterien*.

Poor and unemployed, Vinz, Hubert, and Saïd drift through their day. They visit Hubert's gym which has been destroyed during the riots. The three take the train to Paris to watch a boxing match and for Saïd to collect money from his acquaintance Snoopy. Saïd asks directions from a police officer and runs back to his friends, observing that "The pigs are so fucking polite around here." But politeness has its limits if you are a youth from the *banlieue*. When they come out of Snoopy's luxury apartment, the police have responded to neighbors' complaints. Vinz pretends that he is not part of the group and escapes, but the officers arrest Saïd and Hubert. During the interrogation, the officers taunt them with racial slurs, choke them, and threaten them with a gun.

When the police finally release them, the trains have stopped running. Reunited with Vinz, they go to an art gallery and wonder what the artist did to be famous. Saïd tries to flirt with two Parisian women in the gallery, but he is too aggressive so the gallery owner asks them to leave. Stranded overnight in the streets of Paris, they try to steal a car, but none of them knows how to drive. They learn from watching a TV through the window of a shopping center that Abdel died. In the morning they return to the *banlieue* for the film's violent denouement.

La Haine raises many themes for an ethics of mobility. The film's original title was *Droit de cité*—right of citizenship or, literally, right of the city. This title recalls Henri Lefebrve's classic essay "The Right to the City" which he characterizes as a "cry and a demand" for "a transformed and renewed *right to urban life*" (1996: 158). *La Haine* is an indictment of how many working class people who may also be marginalized because of race or ethnicity are denied this right.

First, the banlieues are physically isolated, separated from the center of the city by location. In many respects, they are not part of Paris or even part of France. In commentary for the Criterion Collection edition of the film, sociologist Sophie Body-Gendrot reports interviewing people who insisted, "I'm not French, I'm from Marseille." Individual identity does not cohere with the French ideal of an undifferentiated *peuple français* united by *liberté*, *fraternité*, and *egalité*. *La Haine* is shot to reflect the differences:

> [Kassovitz] shot the *cité* [Chanteloup-les-Vignes] by day and Paris by night, the *cité* with ample travelling shots and Paris with a small crew (by foot and with a hand-held camera); the *cité* in stereo and Paris in mono. Short focal distance was used for the *cité* scenes, in order to integrate the characters with

their surroundings, whereas Paris is shot with long focal distance to detach them from the background. The result is that, as soon as the protagonists get to Paris, the whole atmosphere and sound changes and they feel out of place and strangers. (Konstantarakos 1999: 163)

Physical isolation is not only (or even principally) a function of distance, but rather a function of public infrastructure—or lack thereof. Since many of the residents rely on public transportation, they are unable to return or leave the neighborhood late at night.

Second, mobility is constrained within the *banlieue*. The police in *La Haine* are an occupying army in Chanteloup-les-Vignes. Indeed, it is hard not to recall Frantz Fanon's observation in *The Wretched of the Earth*:

> The colonized world is a world divided in two. The dividing line, the border, is represented by the barracks and the police stations. In the colonies, the official, legitimate agent, the spokesperson for the colonizer and the regime of oppression, is the police officer or the soldier. (Fanon 2004: 3)

The analogy to French colonialism is not incidental, as many of the residents of the *banlieues* have ancestors from former French colonies. As Loïc Wacquant writes, "how can one not see that those who are designated—indeed defamed—across Europe as 'immigrants' are foreigners of postcolonial origins and lower class extraction while others, of upper-class standing, are 'expats', who everyone wants to attract and not drive out?" (Wacquant 2014: 1688). This community has long suffered institutional violence, including the murder of hundreds of Algerians in France during the Algerian war. The second and third generations of French youth of North African heritage have not forgotten legacy of colonialism which they link to their social and economic exclusion (Body-Gendrot 2010: 659).

This connects to a fourth type of separation by class and ethnicity. Though pundits often attribute social unrest in the *banlieues* to a concentration of supposedly culturally distinct Muslim communities, this is a misperception. Commentators frequently connect the French *banlieues* to the American inner city and compare *La Haine* to Spike Lee's *Do the Right Thing* and John Singleton's *Boyz n the Hood*. But though significant numbers of ethnic and racial minorities tend to live the *banlieues*, the *banlieues* are far more mixed than the US inner city. As *La Haine* suggested, French *banlieues* are not ethnically homogenous and include "old-stock" French residents (Body-Gendrot 2009: 68–8).

Third, mobility is constrained not only by geography and physical force, but also by culture and by symbolic borders. In the art gallery we see the cultural divide and how lack of cultural capital disadvantages the youth from the *banlieue*. A hierarchical education system savagely sorts citizens, reproducing inequalities not only through purchasing power, but through codes of communication that signal belonging (Bourdieu and Passeron 1990).

Cultural markers are reinforced by symbolic markers. Media and politicians frequently attribute unrest to culture, particularly Islam which has been construed as an existential threat to French laïcité. Appearance is used as a means to communicate that Muslims do not belong, as was evident in *L'affaire du foulard* in the early 1990s that banned the hijab from schools. More recently, we had the attempt of French mayors to ban the "burkini"— a full-length swimsuit that covers everything except the face, hands, and feet. These bans are forms of symbolic exclusion with material effects. They do not simply enforce a dress code on Muslim women; they serve to limit their mobility, along with their access to education, employment, and democratic representation. The cruel irony missed by those who see Muslim women in need of saving (Abu-Lughod 2002) is that these bans exclude the women they claim to liberate from the public sphere.

Finally, questions about the *banlieues* are intertwined with broad questions about migration to France and to Europe. We can shift our attention from the *banlieues* to Calais, where thousands of asylum seekers have gathered with the hope of finding passage across the channel to England. French authorities cleared and bulldozed the "jungle"—a shanty town on a former landfill site where many migrants resided—in October 2016 on "humanitarian grounds" (Blamont 2016). Nonetheless, the migrants remain. The French government has vowed not to build a reception center, instead choosing to deploy more riot police (Savary 2017).

From Calais, we should look across the Mediterranean to Libya, where the EU has with limited success tried to co-opt the coastguard into preventing migration (Lewis 2017). From Libya's coasts, we can turn our attention to its detention centers, plagued by arbitrary detention, forced labor, torture, and sexual violence (United Nations Support Mission in Libya 2016). From Libya, we can turn our gaze east to Syria or West to Senegal or South-East to Sudan and Somalia where refugees are forced to circumvent a gauntlet of state-imposed barriers to seek asylum.

What we see are variations on a theme in which people are declared as "other" and excluded. This may take the form of Libyan coastguard officers opening fire on boats (Belhumeur 2017) or French authorities destroying shacks that provided some shelter and dignity to people hoping to reunite with family in England. It can be through detention and deportation or exploitive labor conditions benignly tolerated by authorities who step in to selectively enforce laws against unruly workers. Again Loïc Wacquant is eloquent:

> The selective targeting and preferential confinement of foreigners issued from the West's foreign empires take the two complementary forms of internal and external "transportation"—carceral expurgation and geographic expulsion (dramatized by the bureaucratic-cum-journalistic ceremony of the "charter flight"). They are complemented by the rapid development of a vast network of detention camps reserved for irregular migrants and by aggressive policies of detection and exclusion that incite informality among those migrants and normalize the "misrule of law" across the continent as well as export it to sending countries via the "externalization" of programs of immigration and asylum control. (Wacquant 2014: 1696)

Migration is regulated over a large, transnational system of sometimes independent, sometimes overlapping mechanisms. The complexity of how these migration systems work—keeping in mind to a significant extent they do not function as intended—is daunting. Nonetheless, if we fail to explore the connections, then we will fail to understand migration and fall short in our moral evaluations. Russell King writes:

> barriers to an holistic, synthesizing study of migration are posed by the division of the migration process into its many fragmented component stages (departure, arrival, return) and by the hegemonic role of national models and discourses of immigration and ethnicity (assimilation, integration, multiculturalism, *ius sanguinis*, etc.). (King 2002: 91)

Along with a more holistic, synthesized social science, we need a more complex ethics of migration.

TOWARD A MORE COMPLEX ETHICS OF MOBILITY AND BORDERS

By rejecting methodological nationalism and refusing to address international migration under its lens, we can see old questions from a newer perspective and notice new questions for investigation. If we instead classify international migration within a broader theory of mobility and spatially based exclusion, national borders become just one more type of barrier. Of course, this does not mean that national borders are not important. As Ali Madanipour acknowledges, "no other form of [socio-spatial] exclusion has been associated with such high costs in human life, sacrifice, and misery" (Madanipour 2005: 82). Nonetheless, national borders are not the only means of socio-spatial exclusion: the spatial dimension of social exclusion at the urban and national level has important parallels with exclusion at the international level.

As *La Haine* indicates, the city is one of the central sites where exclusion is carried out. Oddly, the urban dimension of migration control is neglected, especially in the normative literature. Nicholas De Genova writes:

> migrant studies research tends to be disproportionately urban in its empirical orientation, but commonly leaves the urban question profoundly undertheorized, if not utterly unexamined. In part, this shortcoming derives from the degree to which the study of migration has inevitably been framed by the border and immigration regimes of "national" states, leaving the urban spatial setting of most migrants' experiences and practices presupposed as merely the background "context" for struggles that are politically articulated to the national scale. (De Genova 2015: 3)

Taking urbanism and the city seriously for an ethics of migration requires connecting the diverse borders and barriers that affect justice. How immigrants—or groups conceived as immigrants—are treated may affect external admissions policies. For example, links drawn between terrorism and immigration may lead to the exclusion of refugees, even if the evidence does not support connections (Nowrasteh 2016). Furthermore, questions of justice do not end once people have been admitted to the territory. We cannot claim to have just immigration policies if immigrants are physically separated in "ghettos," racially stigmatized, deskilled, and subject to discriminatory policing because they are popularly defined as outside of the community. Immigration policy produces illegality; it also produces precarious forms of inclusion, not only by restricting legal rights (to receive services, to change jobs, to remain), but also by marking people as "foreign." Immigration admissions and the domestic treatment of minority populations are largely conceived independently.

We need richer, more nuanced political philosophy of borders. Baldly stated, this claim faces two sorts of objections. First, theorists from the social sciences may object that political philosophy is superfluous or even ideological. (This worry is not usually voiced in print, but it is sometimes raised in conversation and is confirmed by the paucity of citations to philosophical works in the empirical literature.) Many researchers and activists concerned with migration are convinced that border enforcement is deeply unjust and see little value in political philosophers reaffirming their convictions (and even less value in political philosophers not immersed in the empirical literature or involved in migrant struggles informing them that they are mistaken).

Every day asylum seekers drown in the sea or die by dehydration in the desert, governments callously separate parents and young children, private prison companies lobby to continue to fill their jail cells, and refugees endure in poorly funded camps with little hope of resuming lives of hope and dignity. Surely, governments that actively pursue policies that harm or kill vulnerable people are acting wrongly. Political philosophy adds little to this observation.

More worrisome is the possibility that philosophy sometimes plays an ideological role. On this view, closed border theorists perform scholastic gymnastics to sanitize the everyday violence of border violence as "coercion" and efface relationships of power with the bloodless language of state or community rights. Even open border theorists distanced from thick, phenomenologically rich descriptions are accused of "utopianism" and political irrelevance to more militant struggles.

The second sort of objection comes from political philosophers irked by the suggestion that they have not already developed a sufficiently rich and nuanced philosophy of borders. After all, there are sophisticated literatures on the ethics of border controls, multiculturalism and minority nationalism, segregation and gentrification, and the moral status of state borders (e.g., in the nationalism/statism vs. cosmopolitanism debates). To claim otherwise simply reflects ignorance of the field.

I will deal with these objections in turn. To see where political philosophy has a useful role, consider the call of some activist-scholars for "No Borders" (Anderson et al. 2009; Jones 2016; King 2016). No Borders scholarship calls for social justice movements to "not only 'confront' the question of the border" but also to "*reject* borders that work to multiply both control devices and differentiated labor regimes" (Anderson et al. 2009: 11, italics in original). Many "No Borders" scholars and activists distinguish their position from calls for open borders made on behalf of economic efficiency and the freedom to seek work with the greatest return for human capital. They also distinguish their position from humanitarian cries to open borders to admit people fleeing violence or economic insecurity. The No Borders movement often grounds itself in anarchist and socialist traditions and calls for the radical transformation (if not abolition) of the world economy and state sovereignty.

I share much of their anger and anguish at a deeply unjust system. Nonetheless, political philosophy has a role in sharpening its claims. As should be clear from this brief description, "No Borders" does not literally mean no borders (indeed, it is hard to conceive what this could mean). Rather, it reflects opposition to particular borders imposed by states and by powerful economic actors such as corporations. No Borders activists are well aware that borders allow for the creation and sustainability of the social world. For example, Natasha King has written perceptively about her experience living in a squat on Victor Hugo Street in Calais with women hoping to cross to the United Kingdom. The house served as a haven for migrant women and their children. This created a morally complex (and ambiguous) dynamic in which activist, white European men with papers would prevent black, migrant African men without papers from entering (King 2016).

The point is not that we should condemn exclusion, but rather acknowledge its moral complexity. In this case, there were good reasons for a safe shelter for women and their children, though this came at the cost of excluding equally or even more needy men. What is needed is careful reflection about the morality of exclusion, a task at which political philosophers excel. Borders can produce illegality, but they can also nourish us. Even when they are fluid and porous and communities are diverse and welcoming, borders nonetheless have an exclusionary function. If nothing else, they distinguish insiders from those who have not sought admittance. Even non-territorialized mobile commons need to distribute scarce resources and to exclude police who seek to bring their members under territorial control.

Rather than offering a theory about the ethics of borders, No Borders theorists gain much of their authority from opposing particularly appalling practices. This is effective when injustice is glaring and its diagnosis relies on commonly shared convictions. Outside of injustice that is obvious to most people (which encompasses surprisingly little in an era where the far right has infected mainstream political parties and culture), the No Borders movement is most compelling to people who already share many of its broader sympathies. These sympathies include a rejection of state rights to prevent migration through violent means and a broader skepticism (often anarchist) about state legitimacy and opposition to capitalist markets.

Since these sympathies are not shared by most people, more needs to be done to persuade. Political philosophy becomes important when people's opinions differ and moral status of borders is controversial. Political philosophers offer clarity, distinguishing different moral dimensions and making a case for their salience (or lack thereof). Ideally, they can also bring into dialogue open-minded people who think differently about border controls.

In contrast, political philosophers have developed sophisticated normative theories, but have applied them to an incomplete or impoverished view of borders. There are at least four largely separate literatures in political philosophy that concern borders and mobility.[3] First, political philosophers have examined the moral status (if any) of state territorial borders (Miller 2012; Nine 2012; Simmons 2001). This literature also connects to questions of political secession, asking what moral claims might ground a right of national communities or other groups to secede or deserve special rights over a territory (Buchanan 2003). It also often conceives itself as answering questions about territorial rights which may or may not be connected to the right to regulate migration (Sanderlin 2015).

Second, political philosophers have debated whether borders should be open to international migrants or if states have a moral right to exclude at least some migrants (Wilcox 2009). In this literature, the relationship is primarily between individual migrants and states, though on occasion the interests of individual citizens (e.g., people wishing to sponsor the migration of their family) come into play. The open borders debate primarily concerns state territorial borders with limited reflection on how they interact with other sorts of borders.[4]

Third, political philosophers have debated questions of integration and admission to the political community and the types of legal and symbolic boundaries that can be legitimately imposed. One recent theme is the requirement that people seeking full membership pass citizenship tests (Carens 2013; Honohan 2016). These debates usually assume that the question of admission to the community has been settled, though there is some overlap in discussions about the ethical criteria for regularization of the status of unauthorized immigrants (Carens 2013; Hosein 2016).

Finally, political philosophers have explored questions of segregation and gentrification within cities (Hayward and Swanstrom 2011; Young 2011). In the United States this has mostly focused on African-American communities, a topic that most philosophers have assumed is unrelated to questions of multiculturalism and minority nationalism.[5] In the literature on multiculturalism, the supposed isolation of "ethnic" communities is often framed as a question about the special rights or representation that communities may (or may not) deserve to continue (often religious) practices central to their culture (Kymlicka 1995). The possibility that ethnic communities suffer from economic and social exclusion is for the most part not broached.

It is not possible to begin to do justice to these literatures here, all of which contain vital (as well as diverse and conflicting) insights for thinking about the ethics of borders. Instead, a few remarks must suffice. First, except for discussion on segregation and gentrification (which is usually treated as unrelated to immigration), these literatures all largely treat state borders as the object of analysis or as an invisible backdrop. The literature on territorial borders mostly explains why territorial borders are justified and offers criteria for rejecting some borders or creating new ones (e.g., in the case of secession). The open borders debate asks whether it is permissible to restrict migration across state borders. The multiculturalism literature asks about the relationship of minority cultures and individuals with the national/state community. The literature on segregation and gentrification mostly sees itself as unconnected to migration or to transnationalism. In other words, these debates are conducted under the assumptions of methodological nationalism.

Second, these literatures tend to operate in isolation of each other. Migration and many communities are fluid and cross borders, but these literatures assume that they can be examined within the boundaries of nation-states or neighborhoods. Instead, we need to ask what happens when we examine migration and mobility taking into account multiple levels of analysis. For example, one major argument for opening borders is that it would result in enormous economic gains (Clemens 2011; Pritchett 2006). This is true, but as a matter of ethical analysis, it is incomplete. Studies of internal migration from rural to urban areas suggest that opening borders would leave much inequality intact, if not exacerbate it. Removing de jure exclusion in which the state chooses not to exercise coercion does little to prevent private exclusions based on property rights. Nor does it dispel deep set racist or xenophobic animus or change the ways in which gender skews opportunities. These considerations are not an objection to opening borders, but rather insist that the topic be analyzed in its full complexity.

Criteria for an Ethics of Borders

A theory of borders and mobility should be pluralist. It needs to acknowledge that there are many types of borders and that borders interact. It should also recognize that borders are productive—by drawing borders around people we create communities and enable them to create and protect goods. Borders can justly exclude, but the onus of proof should be on those who justify exclusion. When examining borders, we should ask, What ends does the border serve? Who is excluded? Why are they excluded? How they are excluded is also vitally important. Even if migration restrictions are justified, the violence of many migration controls is morally unacceptable (Jones 2016; Sager 2017).

What resources are available to guide us in our moral evaluations given the complexity of the topic? I suggest that our approach should be critically cosmopolitan and that Amartya Sen's capability approach provides useful guidance for assessing border regimes. Moreover, a theory of just borders should be acutely aware of relationships of domination and hierarchy and eschew institutions and mechanisms that mark people as unequal and curtail their opportunities.

Critical Cosmopolitanism

My first suggestion is that we should adopt a critical cosmopolitan stance. If we reduce cosmopolitanism to a conviction that every person has equal moral worth, almost every political philosopher claims to be a cosmopolitan. By critical cosmopolitanism, I have three claims in mind (Delanty 2012). First, critical cosmopolitanism takes seriously social scientific research that takes a cosmopolitan stance. In particular, it draws on criticisms of sedentariness from the mobility paradigm and attempts to think past methodological nationalism by drawing attention to globalism, transnationalism, and banal cosmopolitanism. Critical cosmopolitanism is critical of the explanatory adequacy of nationalist ontology that distorts so much work in the social sciences.

Second, social scientific cosmopolitanism is connected to moral cosmopolitanism. The emergence of cosmopolitan connections or institutions supports a cosmopolitan morality by revealing causal links and webs of responsibility. Critical cosmopolitanism insists on the equal moral worth of all people and is skeptical of any justifications for institutions that provide people with sharply different opportunities. It does not necessarily rail against mobility restrictions, but they must be justified to those who find their movement impeded.

This ethics is cosmopolitan in the sense that people matter equally, but it is not crudely universalistic or individualistic. Commitment to the moral equality of all human beings is fundamental, but when it is combined with the moral individualism of most human rights accounts, it can fail to fully capture the wrongness of most mobility restrictions.[6] We need to be sensitive to how mobility restrictions serve to uphold inequalities, maintain privilege, and extract rents. Individualistic human rights-based approaches eschew class-based analysis of international migration in which skilled workers are often actively recruited, temporary workers are tolerated under often adverse conditions, and many others can only migrate clandestinely. It also overlooks the role of patriarchy and of racism in unjust institutions that contribute to harming migrants. Critical cosmopolitanism is opposed to hierarchy and domination and to the silencing of significant parts of the human population.

Third, critical cosmopolitanism has an emancipatory aim: by criticizing certain types of borders and mobility restrictions, it seeks to find more inclusive alternatives. Critical cosmopolitans should seek to understand the world *and to shape it.* Critical cosmopolitanism comes with a moral imperative to try to contribute to bringing into the world arrangements and institutions that fulfill cosmopolitan requirements. Mobility is not only restricted by immigration laws. It is also structured by property rights. As Thomas Nail puts it, "The ownership of private property is not simply a social inequality but also a kinetic inequality" (Nail 2016: 141). Critical cosmopolitanism seeks to understand how borders affect welfare and opportunities and determine their justice. If unjust, it searches for alternative arrangements.

In exploring the implications of critical cosmopolitanism for borders, we can take a cue from Robert Goodin's analysis of compatriot priority. Compatriot priority tells us that it is just or even morally required to give priority to the welfare of fellow citizens over foreigners. It contends that we have special obligations to compatriots, just as we have special obligations to family, friends, co-workers, benefactors, and others. These special obligations have been invoked by those who argue for treating co-citizens better than people generally (e.g., we should give more weight to the poverty of co-citizens than the poverty of people living in other countries).

In response to theorists who insist on these special obligations, Goodin pointed out that the treatment of compatriots is decidedly mixed. In many cases, we are obligated to treat foreigners *better* that compatriots. Fellow citizens are routinely taxed and conscripted. They may have their property seized through eminent domain or find themselves exposed to harm from products that we could not sell abroad (Goodin 1988: 668–669). How, then, do we explain the widespread conviction that we have special duties to treat people in our national community better?

Goodin's response is that special duties toward co-nationals are simply an efficient way of assigning responsibility for general duties toward humans more generally. According to his account, "special duties derive the whole of their moral force from the moral force of those general duties" (Goodin 1988: 679). Nonetheless, in order to discharge these general duties, it is useful to assign special responsibility to some individuals or groups. National boundaries may be justified, but only if their division of labor is effective in fulfilling general duties. He writes, "Boundaries matter, I conclude. But it is the boundaries around people, not the boundaries around territories, that really matter morally" (Goodin 1988: 686).

Goodin's focus is national boundaries, but his account is much broader, entailing that we should draw and redraw boundaries to promote human flourishing. Associations and communities are important since we become fully human by communing with others. However, they do not line up with nation-states. Many of them cross international borders, especially migration systems that intimately link people who often do not notice their corresponding moral responsibilities.

In evaluating the multiple borders that structure human lives, John Agnew evinces a normative commitment "that the answer of what borders do should always be related to the overriding ethical concern that they serve and not undermine human dignity and what Jonathan Seglow has called 'the right to a decent life'" (Agnew 2008: 176; c.f. Seglow 2005). Critical cosmopolitanism seeks a decent life for all.

Capabilities

This brings us to questions about the metric of justice. How do we understand a decent life? Amartya Sen's capabilities approach is particularly amenable to evaluating the role of borders (Nussbaum 2008; Sen 2008, 2011). The capability approach emphasizes how individual, social, and environmental differences affect people's freedom and well-being.[7] We can understand people's capabilities as a function of their abilities, their resources, and their physical and social environments. Natural capacities, resources, and the environment interact in complex ways in determining people's capabilities. In many cases, justice requires the construction of an environment that allows people to flourish. Capabilities are never a matter of an individual's attributes, but always are realized in relationship with the environment (including the social and legal environments). For example, the mobility of someone in a wheelchair depends on the physical environment.

If we evaluate migration in terms of capabilities, mobility is a dimension that interacts with place and other resources to allow people to exercise their capabilities. The capabilities approach would take seriously Michael Clemens and Lant Pritchett's insistence that "people matter more than patches of earth," as well as their observation that how well people do is in part a function of their relationship to patches of earth (Clemens and Pritchett 2008). Clemens and Pritchett ingeniously replace income per resident (a methodologically nationalist metric that measures development by looking at people currently residing within a national territory) with per person income (which looks at the income of a person born in a given country regardless of where they now reside). They conclude that this shifting perspective shows migration *is* development.

The nation-state still plays a central role in Clemens and Pritchett's account, albeit a more nuanced role that better reflects development: per person income captures the rise in income when a Haitian moves to the United States. There is no a priori reason, though, to insist that nation-states fix the boundaries when we are investigating human freedom and well-being. For example, it might suit some purposes to ask what happens when Haitians move from Port-au-Prince to Miami. Or our interest may be how people's capabilities change when they move from rural to urban settings, inner cities to suburbs, or Export-Processing Zones to global cities. The right unit of analysis depends on our goals.

What the capabilities approach tells us is that we should structure borders to promote real opportunities for people to act in ways that increase their freedom and welfare. David Harvey points out that "those who define the material practices, forms, and meaning of money, time, or space, fix certain basic rules of the social game" (Harvey 1989: 226). Critical cosmopolitanism asks who is fixing the rules, who benefits, and how we could do better in allowing as many people as possible to enjoy a full life.

Domination and Hierarchy

Though the capability approach follows methodological individualism in that individuals' capabilities are what matter morally, the assessment of institutions and policies needs to evaluate how groups are affected. In particular, we need to resist institutions that permit domination and illegitimate hierarchies. A just distribution of capabilities must not allow some groups to exercise arbitrary power over others (Pettit 1997).[8]

Nor should institutions embody structural injustice by systematically limiting the opportunities and freedom of some groups on morally arbitrary grounds. Exclusion may be economic, political, and cultural (Madanipour 2005). Economic exclusion primarily concerns access to resources such as employment, whereas political exclusion concerns access to decision-making. Cultural exclusion concerns access to common narratives. Barriers can be physical, legal, or symbolic. There are also psychological barriers where people choose not to seek opportunities because they believe—rightly or wrongly—they will not be accepted.

We should be particularly adverse to forms of differential inclusion and exclusion. Maribel Casa-Cortes draws attention to the work of Stuart Hall who theorized how "specific, differentiated forms of *incorporation* have consistently been associated with the appearance of racist, ethnically segmentary and other similar social features" (Hall 1986: 25; cited in Casa-Cortes et al. 2015: 25). We need to avoid "categorical inequalities" in which negative social categorizations enshrined in laws, policies, customs, and symbols allow for exploitation and opportunity hoarding (Tilly 1999). Of particular importance is the way in which class-stratification, racialization, and sexism systematically exclude some people (Bauman 2001; Massey 2007).

What is most problematic about migration controls is the violence used in preventing and shaping movement and the lack of say that most migrants have in the institutions that regulate their lives. Contemporary border controls combine domination—nation-states exercise arbitrary power over migrants (Abizadeh 2008; Sager 2017)—with opportunity hoarding (Tilly 1999). They also frequently play a role in expelling parts of the population (Sassen 2014), most brutally when nation-building demands the expulsion of ethnic minorities.

Studies of nationalism and multiculturalism reveal how nation-building projects have constructed imaginary communities through the suppression and denationalization of indigenous and selected immigrant groups (Ngai 2004; Volpp 2015). When looking at migration, mobility, and borders we should be particularly sensitive to their origins and how they are maintained. Political philosophers too often fail to consider the history of border construction. Jennifer Pitts writes:

> With Rawls, the literature on contemporary cosmopolitanism has tended to ask how liberal states and societies should respond to the pathologies they encounter out there, and how they might intervene to promote democracy, rather than taking the prosperous and relatively stable societies of the global north and the impoverished and too often authoritarian states of the global south as products of the same long history of asymmetrical interaction and mutual constitution. (Pitts 2010: 222)

History reminds us of how borders have actually been constructed, in many cases by imperial powers and colonial administrators with indifference to existing communal boundaries of many people.

Conclusion: La Haine Revisited

To a critical cosmopolitan, what stands out most sharply when we turn our gaze to the *banlieues* or the destitute migrants in Calais are domination and hierarchy. In the Chanteloup-les-Vignes of *La Haine*, working class people—often with parents or grandparents who migrated to France from former colonies—find themselves systematically excluded from opportunities and constantly reminded that authorities can and will exercise arbitrary power over their lives. In Calais, we see how the lack of papers condemns asylum seekers to the margins, at least temporarily immobilized by a border wall, armed guards, and legal prohibitions. If we look beyond the Mediterranean to refugees in Libya, a global regime of migration controls becomes visible that has aptly been compared to a feudal regime of birthright privilege (Carens 1987) or a global version of apartheid (Moses 2006).

We should ask ourselves if our current borders regimes indeed promote human flourishing. What is their role in assuring or denying people a reasonable set of capabilities? How do borders, territory, and mobility interact to determine people's life chances? What alternatives are available that would allow for security and prosperity, but also assign responsibilities so that vulnerable people are embraced rather than illegalized and persecuted?

These are difficult questions. What I am confident about is that they cannot be answered from a methodological nationalist stance. If we analyze the world as a set of as nation-states characterized as sealed, sovereign containers, we will fail to understand migration and the forces that lead people to move. Moreover, we will fail to recognize the injustice of many of these forces and the relationships of responsibility many people have toward those who find themselves violently excluded.

Notes

1. Approximately 15 serious clashes between youth and police occurred between the start of the 1980s and 2010 (Body-Gendrot 2010: 660).
2. "Banlieue" refers to a suburb of a city, but it is more akin to the US inner city.
3. A related debate concerns the criteria for determining the scope of the democratic community, sometimes in terms of the "boundary problem" in political philosophy that asks how we can determine the scope of the demos. For a sample of this literature, see Abizadeh (2012), Bauböck (2007), Goodin (2007), Lopez-Guerra (2005), and Sager (2014).
4. An exception is Michael Walzer's suggestion that it is necessary to regulate movement across state borders in order that neighborhoods remain open. Walzer provocatively asserts that "To tear down the walls of the state is not, as Sidgwick worriedly suggested, to create a world without walls, but rather to create a thousand petty fortresses" (Walzer 1983: 39). Walzer raises an important issue about the interaction of types of borders but does not pursue it very far and offers little evidence that open borders would indeed lead to "a thousand petty fortresses." He also neglects the extent that many petty fortresses do in fact exist and are at least partly the result of state borders (e.g., due to their role in illegalizing ethnic and racialized groups).
5. A notable exception that connects these two literatures is Valls (2010).
6. By moral individualism, I am not disputing that morality ultimately derives from the well-being of individuals. Rather, I refer to the failure to analyze people as members of groups. For example, it makes a difference if someone has fewer opportunities because of structural racism.
7. Sen proposed capabilities as an alternative to welfare-based and resource-based approaches to distributive justice (Sen 1980). Welfare-based approaches that focus on individuals' subjective evaluations of their well-being are vulnerable to the charge of "adaptive preferences"—for example, some groups may be socialized to be content with a subordinate position (Nussbaum 2008). Proponents of the capabilities approach hold that the

advantage of focusing on capabilities over resources is that capabilities specify the *ends* themselves. Resource-based approaches instead target *means* to unspecified ends. An advantage of capabilities approach is that it refocuses away attention from distribution—who gets what—to questions of what people can actually do and enjoy.
8. In the previous work I have developed the implications for neo-republican accounts of freedom as non-domination for political inclusion and for the ethics of migration policy (Sager 2014, 2017).

References

Abizadeh, A. 2008. Democratic Theory and Border Coercion: No Right to Unilaterally Control Your Own Borders. *Political Theory* 36 (1): 37–65.

Abizadeh, Arash. 2012. On the Demos and Its Kin: Nationalism, Democracy, and the Boundary Problem. *American Political Science Review* 106 (4): 867–882.

Abu-Lughod, Lila. 2002. Do Muslim Women Really Need Saving? Anthropological Reflections on Cultural Relativism and Its Others. *American Anthropologist* 104 (3): 783–790. https://doi.org/10.1525/aa.2002.104.3.783.

Agnew, John. 2008. Borders on the Mind: Re-framing Border Thinking. *Ethics & Global Politics* 1 (4): 175–191.

Anderson, Bridget, Nandita Sharma, and Cynthia Wright. 2009. Editorial: Why No Borders? *Refuge* 26 (2): 5–17.

Bauböck, Rainer. 2007. Stakeholder Citizenship and Transnational Political Participation: A Normative Evaluation of External Voting. *Fordham Law Review* 75: 2393–2447.

Bauman, Zygmunt. 2001. *Globalization: The Human Consequences.* New York: Columbia University Press.

Belhumeur, Jenna. 2017. Libyan Coastguard Opened Fire at Refugee Boats: NGOs. *Al Jazeera*, May 25. http://www.aljazeera.com/news/2017/05/libyan-coastguard-opens-fire-migrant-boats-ngos-170525100451559.html

Blamont, Matthias. 2016. France Clears 'Jungle' Migrant Camp in Calais, Children in Limbo. *Reuters*, October 24. http://www.reuters.com/article/us-europe-migrants-calais-idUSKCN12O0JN

Body-Gendrot, Sophie. 2009. A Plea for Urban Disorder: A Plea for Urban Disorder. *The British Journal of Sociology* 60 (1): 65–73.

———. 2010. Police Marginality, Racial Logics and Discrimination in the *Banlieues* of France. *Ethnic and Racial Studies* 33 (4): 656–674.

Bourdieu, Pierre, and Jean Claude Passeron. 1990. *Reproduction in Education, Society, and Culture.* 1990 ed. London and Newbury Park, CA: Sage Publications.

Buchanan, Allen. 2003. *Justice, Legitimacy, and Self-Determination.* Oxford: Oxford University Press.

Carens, Joseph H. 1987. Aliens and Citizens: The Case for Open Borders. *Review of Politics* 49 (2): 251–273.
———. 2013. *The Ethics of Immigration*. New York: Oxford University Press.
Casas-Cortes, Maribel, et al. 2015. New Keywords: Migration and Borders. *Cultural Studies* 29 (1): 55–87.
Clemens, Michael A. 2011. Economics and Emigration: Trillion-Dollar Bills on the Sidewalk? *Journal of Economic Perspectives* 25 (3): 83–106. https://doi.org/10.1257/jep.25.3.83.
Clemens, Michael A., and Lant Pritchett. 2008. Income per Natural: Measuring Development for People Rather Than Places. *Population and Development Review* 34 (3): 395–434.
De Genova, Nicholas. 2015. Border Struggles in the Migrant Metropolis. *Nordic Journal of Migration Research* 5 (1): 3–10.
Delanty, Gerard. 2012. The Idea of Critical Cosmopolitanism. In *Routledge Handbook of Cosmopolitanism Studies*, ed. Gerard Delanty, 38–46. Routledge International Handbooks. Abingdon, Oxon and New York: Routledge.
Fanon, Frantz. 2004. *The Wretched of the Earth*. Translated by Richard Philcox. New York: Grove Press.
Goodin, Robert E. 1988. What Is So Special About Our Fellow Countrymen? *Ethics* 98 (4): 663–686.
———. 2007. Enfranchising All Affected Interests, and Its Alternatives. *Philosophy & Public Affairs* 35 (1): 40–68. https://doi.org/10.1111/j.1088-4963.2007.00098.x.
Hall, S. 1986. Gramsci's Relevance for the Study of Race and Ethnicity. *Journal of Communication Inquiry* 10 (2): 5–27.
Harvey, David. 1989. *The Condition of Postmodernity*. Cambridge, MA: Basil Blackwell.
Hayward, Clarissa Rile, and Todd Swanstrom, eds. 2011. *Justice and the American Metropolis*. Globalization and Community, v. 18. Minneapolis: University of Minnesota Press.
Honohan, Iseult. 2016. Civic Integration: The Acceptable Face of Assimilation? In *The Ethics and Politics of Immigration: Core Issues and Emerging Trends*, ed. Alex Sager, 145–158. Lanham: Rowman & Littlefield International.
Hosein, Adam. 2016. Arguments for Regularization. In *The Ethics and Politics of Immigration: Core Issues and Emerging Trends*, ed. Alex Sager, 159–179. Lanham: Rowman & Littlefield International.
Jones, Reece. 2016. *Violent Borders: Refugees and the Right to Move*. London and New York: Verso.
King, Russell. 2002. Towards a New Map of European Migration. *International Journal of Population Geography* 8 (2): 89–106. https://doi.org/10.1002/ijpg.246.
King, Natasha. 2016. *No Borders: The Politics of Immigration Control and Resistance*. London: Zed Books.

Konstantarakos, Myrto. 1999. La Haine and the Cinéma de Banlieue. In *French Cinema in the 1990s: Continuity and Difference: Essays*, ed. Phil Powrie, 160–171. Oxford and New York: Oxford University Press.

Kymlicka, Will. 1995. *Multicultural Citizenship: A Liberal Theory of Minority Rights*. Oxford Political Theory. Oxford and New York: Clarendon Press and Oxford University Press.

Lefebvre, Henri. 1996. In *Writings on Cities*, ed. Eleonore Kofman and Elizabeth Lebas. Cambridge, MA: Blackwell Publishers.

Lewis, Aiden. 2017. EU Effort to Halt Migrants Founders in Libya's Chaos. *Reuters*, June 26. http://www.reuters.com/article/us-europe-migrants-libya-idUSKBN19H0MB

Lopez-Guerra, Claudio. 2005. Should Expatriates Vote? *Journal of Political Philosophy* 13 (2): 216–234.

Madanipour, Ali. 2005. Social Exclusion and Space. In *Social Exclusion in European Cities: Processes, Experiences and Responses*, ed. Ali Madanipour, Göran Cars, and Judith Allen, 75–89. London: Routledge.

Massey, Douglas S. 2007. *Categorically Unequal: The American Stratification System*. A Russell Sage Foundation Centennial Volume. New York: Russell Sage Foundation.

Miller, David. 2012. Territorial Rights: Concept and Justification. *Political Studies* 60 (2): 252–268.

Moses, Jonathon Wayne. 2006. *International Migration: Globalization's Last Frontier*. Global Issues. New York, NY: Zed Books.

Nail, Thomas. 2016. *Theory of the Border*. Oxford and New York: Oxford University Press.

Ngai, Mae M. 2004. *Impossible Subjects: Illegal Aliens and the Making of Modern America*. Princeton, NJ: Princeton University Press.

Nine, Cara. 2012. *Global Justice and Territory*. Oxford, UK: Oxford University Press.

Nowrasteh, Alex. 2016. Terrorism and Immigration: A Risk Analysis. Policy Analysis 798. Cato Institute. https://object.cato.org/sites/cato.org/files/pubs/pdf/pa798_2.pdf

Nussbaum, Martha C. 2008. *Women and Human Development: The Capabilities Approach*. 13. Print. The John Robert Seeley Lectures 3. Cambridge: Cambridge University Press.

Pettit, Philip. 1997. *Republicanism: A Theory of Freedom and Government*. Oxford Political Theory. Oxford and New York: Clarendon Press and Oxford University Press.

Pitts, Jennifer. 2010. Political Theory of Empire and Imperialism. *Annual Review of Political Science* 13: 211–235.

Pritchett, Lant. 2006. *Let Their People Come: Breaking the Gridlock on International Labor Mobility*. Washington, DC and Baltimore, MD: Center for Global Development and Distributed by Brookings Institution Press.

Sager, Alex. 2014. Political Rights, Republican Freedom, and Temporary Workers. *Critical Review of International Social and Political Philosophy* 17 (2): 189–211.
———. 2017. Immigration Enforcement and Domination: An Indirect Argument for Much More Open Borders. *Political Research Quarterly* 70 (1): 42–54.
Sandelind, Clara. 2015. Territorial Rights and Open Borders. *Critical Review of International Social and Political Philosophy* 18 (5): 487–507.
Sassen, Saskia. 2014. *Expulsions: Brutality and Complexity in the Global Economy*. Cambridge, MA: The Belknap Press of Harvard University Press.
Savary, Pierre. 2017. Amid Criticism from Rights Group, France Talks Tough on Calais Migrants. *Reuters*, June 23. http://www.reuters.com/article/us-europe-migrants-calais-idUSKBN19E0V2
Seglow, Jonathan. 2005. The Ethics of Immigration. *Political Studies Review* 3 (3): 317–334.
Sen, Amartya. 1980. Equality of What? In *The Tanner Lecture on Human Values*, I: 197–220. Cambridge: Cambridge University Press.
———. 2008. *Commodities and Capabilities*. New Delhi: Oxford University Press.
———. 2011. *The Idea of Justice*. Cambridge, MA: Harvard University Press.
Simmons, A.J. 2001. On the Territorial Rights of States. *Philosophical Issues: Social, Political, and Legal Philosophy* 11: 300–326.
Tilly, Charles. 1999. *Durable Inequality*. Berkeley: University of California Press.
United Nations Support Mission in Libya. 2016. *Detained and Dehumanised: Report on Human Rights Abuses Against Migrants in Libya*. United Nations Human Rights. https://unsmil.unmissions.org/Portals/unsmil/Documents/Migrants%20report-EN.pdf
Valls, Andrew. 2010. A Liberal Defense of Black Nationalism. *American Political Science Review* 104 (3): 467–481.
Volpp, Leti. 2015. The Indigenous as Alien. *University of California Irvine Law Review* 5: 289–326.
Wacquant, Loïc. 2014. Marginality, Ethnicity and Penality in the Neo-Liberal City: An Analytic Cartography. *Ethnic and Racial Studies* 37 (10): 1687–1711.
Walzer, Michael. 1983. *Spheres of Justice: A Defense of Pluralism and Equality*. New York, NY: Basic Books.
Wilcox, Shelley. 2009. The Open Borders Debate on Immigration. *Philosophy Compass* 4 (5): 813–821.
Young, Iris Marion. 2011. *Justice and the Politics of Difference*. Paperback reissue. Princeton, NJ: Princeton University Press.

CHAPTER 6

Toward a Political Philosophy of Mobility

Abstract The final chapter proposes that abandoning methodological nationalism means that an ethics of immigration is untenable. Rather, what is needed is an ethics of migration or an ethics of mobility that sees movement across state borders, movement within states, and movement to and from cities as raising the same normative issues. In particular, an investigation of the causes of mobility shows that it is often a response to social, economic, and political forces that expel vulnerable people from their homes. The chapter ends with a plea that people recognize the complex ways in which people are connected within and across borders and the dangers of uncritically using words that encourage seeing the world in terms of "us" and "them."

Keywords Ethics of mobility • Identity • Methodological nationalism • Professional ethics • Urbanism

Those with the privilege to carry out academic research have a duty to reflect carefully on their vocation. While the impact of social scientists—let alone political philosophers—is usually limited (at least in the short term), they nonetheless play a role in reifying and legitimizing policies and structures. Borders gain their reality from how we think about them which in turn determines their nature. Walls are insignificant compared to the mental barriers that separate us from our neighbors. Today, border controls condemn millions of people to death, serious harm, and diminished life chances. This is the grim context in which we write books and journal articles and we must ask how our contributions resist or perpetrate injustice.

Ruben Andersson, reflecting on the process that led to his groundbreaking ethnography *Illegality, Inc.* (2014), writes:

> As one leader of a repatriate association told me: "There's lots of money in illegal migration"—not, he specified for the immobile former boat migrants at the center of the visitors' manifold attentions, but rather for state officials and border officers, for researchers and reporters churning out studies and documentaries, and for NGOs keen to set up spurious aid projects with the development money that was now pouring into the region. (2016: 91)

Just as NGO workers and ethnographers must confront ethical questions about their practices and purposes, political philosophers need to consider their roles and methodologies. The effect of political philosophy on the world today is usually modest. Nonetheless, the categories we use for normative analysis are significant. John Maynard Keynes was surely right that "The ideas of economists and political philosophers, both when they are right and when they are wrong, are more powerful than is commonly understood" (1936: 383).

My investigation has been about the categories we should and should not use to think about migration and borders, not what we should think about particular borders and mobility restrictions. It is offered as a prelude to more substantive normative work in ethics and political philosophy. Nonetheless, there are important implications for how we should think about some of the major moral issues surrounding migration.

Perhaps most radically for political philosophy, we should not have an ethics of *immigration* at all. If we choose to write about immigration, we should explicitly acknowledge that we are simplifying matters and ask ourselves carefully if our simplifications distort our moral judgments. In many cases, our topic should be *migration*, exploring how migrants travel within transnational systems that connect people across land, ocean, and air. More often, we should take our departure from a broad ethics of *mobility* that encompasses everything from voyages across continents to moves to a new neighborhood.

Furthermore, once we reject methodological nationalism and the bias toward stasis, many of the issues associated with immigration are not about immigration at all. More precisely, framing the issue as an "immigration issue" obscures what a more fine-grained analysis would reveal as an issue of segregation, coercively imposed inequality, asymmetrical power, or opportunity. The bare fact that someone is a migrant usually has little to no normative import. Instead, we need to see how people are situated in webs of power and hierarchies of inclusion and exclusion. We will often find that whether or not somebody moved or remained within the neighborhood of her birth has no moral salience. Instead, the fact that someone comes from another country is a convenient marker that allows political entrepreneurs to pit immigrants against other marginalized groups.

A second implication when we look at the causes of mobility, including economic transformation, is that it becomes untenable to see forced migration as the exception rather than the rule. International law and nation-states attempt to impose a sharp distinction between refugees fleeing persecution and the so-called economic migrants pursuing opportunities (Ceriani Cernadas 2016). Though many researchers acknowledge the blurred boundaries of this distinction, it continues to play a major role in how migration is conceived.

In contrast, a more perspicuous way of thinking about migration is to think of it as occurring on a spectrum. On one end of the spectrum migration is non-voluntary and only undertaken for survival. On the other end, migration is freely chosen as an idiosyncratic preference, exchanging security and prosperity in one region for similar opportunities in another. Though it is difficult to quantify the "voluntariness" of decisions to migrate, it is likely that they tend to cluster toward the "non-voluntary" part of the spectrum. After all, we live in a world where many endorse the use of violence to keep people in their place. These remarks on the voluntariness of migration also include internal migration—people do not move from rural to urban areas simply looking for opportunity; they move because of structural changes in the economy that have moved the opportunities to cities. Normative theorists have the tripartite task of understanding what leads people to move, determining whether the causes are morally acceptable, and imagining alternative ways of conceiving borders and boundaries that are less coercive and lead to more human flourishing.

A third implication is that we should connect philosophy of the city to the political philosophy of migration. As we have seen in recent months, many of the challenges to the Trump administration's Muslim ban and indiscriminate deportation dragnets have come from cities (Greenwood 2017). Many of the most pressing challenges raised by migration don't primarily concern people crossing international borders. Rather, they concern people moving from rural areas to cities that are often unprepared for the influx. In many cities, police and soldiers remove squatters without legal property rights, destroying their homes. Even when the urban poor have property rights, they are often unable to exercise them or receive only minimal compensation for the destruction of their homes and neighborhoods. This should be understood in terms of forced migration and internal displacement.

Moreover, immigrants predominately move to urban centers where they often compose a significant part of the population. In many respects, placing power over migration in the hands of nation-state conflicts with the needs of migrants and of cities. From the perspective of justice, it is quixotic that people in regions with few migrants can cast a determining vote on immigration policy. Moreover, at the level of the city, the voices of migrants are more likely to reach sympathetic ears among neighbors and representatives.

I end with a plea. Migrants are often called strangers, outsiders. They are often thought—usually without evidence—to possess different cultures, values, and ways of life. Politicians and some philosophers call for protection of *our* culture, *our* values, *our* way of life, oblivious to their narrow conception of the first-person plural. Appeals to culture are used to restrict immigration and discipline migrants with citizenship tests, as well as to subject them to an oppressive regime of mobility restrictions, including detention and deportation.

We should take care when we invoke the words "we" and "our" or when we talk of "us" and "them." This leads people to exclude compatriots who do belong such as the youth from the *banlieue*, even if our societies have regulated these compatriots to the margins of the favored community. It also distracts from our common humanity and the ways that our lives are bound together across borders.

To ignore these commonalities puts us at risk of committing grave injustices. Reflecting on the massacres during the last years of the British Raj in the 1940s and in Rwanda in the mid-1990s, Amartya Sen decries the "illusion of a single identity" that enabled these senseless slaughters. He writes:

It is not remarkable that generating the illusion of unique identity, exploitable for the purpose of confrontation, would appeal to those who are in the business of fomenting violence, and there is no mystery in the fact that such reductionism is sought. But there is a big question about why the cultivation of singularity is so successful, given the extraordinary naïveté of that thesis in a world of obviously plural affiliations. (Sen 2006: 175)

One part of the answer to why the cultivation of singularity is so successful is the success of nation-building over the last two centuries. Nationalism is banal, so much so that we hardly notice it. Criticizing methodological nationalism should awaken us to how strange and untenable it is to organize our vision of the world predominantly around states. The world is much richer, much more diverse than nationalists allow and we are much more connected to each other. An ethics of borders must shake off the blinders of this nationalist vision in favor of cosmopolitanism, in all of its ambiguity and complexity. Only then can we convincingly incorporate mobility and borders into our political philosophy.

References

Andersson, Ruben. 2014. *Illegality, Inc.: Clandestine Migration and the Business of Bordering Europe*. California Series in Public Anthropology 28. Oakland, CA: University of California Press.

Andersson, Ruben. 2016. Europe's Failed 'Fight' Against Irregular Migration: Ethnographic Notes on a Counterproductive Industry. *Journal of Ethnic and Migration Studies* 42 (7): 1055–1075. https://doi.org/10.1080/1369183X.2016.1139446.

Ceriani Cernadas, Pablo. 2016. Language as a Migration Policy Tool. *The Sur File on Migration and Human Rights* 13 (29): 97–111.

Greenwood, Max. 2017. Mayors File Court Brief Opposing Trump's Travel Ban. *The Hill*, March 15. http://thehill.com/blogs/blog-briefing-room/news/324043-city-mayors-file-friend-of-the-court-brief-opposing-trumps

Keynes, John Maynard. 1936. *General Theory of Employment, Interest, and Money*. London: Macmillan.

Sen, Amartya. 2006. *Identity and Violence: The Illusion of Destiny*. 1st ed. Issues of Our Time. New York: W. W. Norton & Co.

REFERENCES

American Civil Liberties Union. n.d. The Constitution in the 100-Mile Border Zone. https://www.aclu.org/other/constitution-100-mile-border-zone
Bauböck, Rainer. 2007. Stakeholder Citizenship and Transnational Political Participation: A Normative Evaluation of External Voting. *Fordham Law Review* 75: 2393–2447.
———. 2010. Cold Constellations and Hot Identities: Political Theory Questions about Transnationalism and Diaspora. In *Diaspora and Transnationalism: Concepts, Theories and Methods*, ed. Rainer Bauböck and Thomas Faist, 295–321. Amsterdam: Amsterdam University Press.
Rushdie, Salman. 1991. *Imaginary Homelands*. New York, NY: Granta.
Waldron, Jeremy. 1991. Minority Cultures and the Cosmopolitan Alternative. *University of Michigan Journal of Law Reform* 25: 751–792.

Index[1]

A
African-American communities, 78–79
Agnew, John, 82
Andersson, Ruben, 22, 92
Anti-nomadic bias, 39
Anti-racism, 27
Armed border guards, 2
Asylum seekers, 73, 76, 85

B
Balibar, Étienne, 8, 46, 47
Banal nationalism, 49n2
Banlieues youth, 70–73
Barbed wire fences, 2
Bauböck, Rainer, viii
Beck, Ulrich, 10, 19, 40, 49n2
Berlin wall, 45
Billig, Michael, 49n2
Blake, Michael, 26, 30n5
Body-Gendrot, Sophie, 71
Borders, 8, 9, 46
    categories of people and identities, 46
    controls, 10, 91, 92
    enforcement, 22
    ethics, criteria of, 80
    studies, 7–9, 45, 47
    walls, 45
Brain drain, 31n14, 61
    emigration of skilled workers, 27
Brettel, Caroline, ixn3
Brown, Wendy, 21, 28
Burkini, 73

C
Calais, 73, 77, 85
Capabilities approach, 86n7
    in borders, 82–84
Carens, Joseph H., vii, ixn1, 6, 13n2, 24–26, 30n5, 30n6, 30n8, 31n13
Casa-Cortes, Maribel, 84
Castles, Stephen, 22, 37, 54, 55
Causality, 54
Channel Tunnel, 21
Chanteloup-les-Vignes, 70–72, 85
Chart routes migrants, 46

---

[1] Note: Page numbers followed by "n" refers to notes.

Circular migration, 26, 28, 45
Citizenship, vii, 8, 22, 23, 43, 44, 47, 63
  right to, 71
  semi-, 63
  tests, 78, 94
Clemens, Michael, 31n14, 83
Cole, Phillip, vii, 24, 26, 30n5, 30n7
Collyer, Michael, 43
Colonialism, 18, 22, 39, 43, 55, 72, 85
Community, 5–7, 10, 11, 12n1, 18–20, 23, 28, 29, 57–59, 72, 75, 76, 78, 79, 82, 86n3, 94
Compatriot priority, 5, 9, 58, 59, 81, 82, 94
Constitution Free Zone, 21
Cosmopolitan, 2
  borders, 9
  social science, 38–41
Cosmopolitanism, 9–12, 40, 76, 85, 95
  banal, 40, 80
  critical, 5, 9, 40, 80–83
Criminal record, 8
Criterion Collection, 71
Critical cosmopolitanism, 5, 9–12, 40, 69–87
Cultural exclusion, 84
Customs and Border Protection (CBP), 21

D
Dangerous classes, 22
Dangerous peoples, 22
Dauvergne, Catherine, 7
David, Charles-Philippe, 45
De Genova, Nicholas, 3, 75
Deportation, 8, 27, 29, 62, 63, 74, 94
Detention, 4, 8, 27, 29, 46, 63, 73, 74, 94
  centers, 21, 73
Development and migration, 4, 18, 25, 28, 83, 92
Dispossession, 56
Division of labor, 82
Domestic workers, 11
Domination, 80, 81, 84, 85
Dreamers, 48
Droit de cité, 71
Dual citizenship, 22, 43
Dumitru, Speranta, 30n3
Dummett, Ann, 30n7

E
Economic exclusion, 72, 84
Economic migrants, 93
Emigrants, 21, 27
Ethics of Immigration (Carens), 13n2, 26, 30n8
Ethnic minorities, 22, 44, 84
Ethnographers, 92
Eurocentrism, 30n12
European Union, 44, 73
  internal borders, 21
Exploitation, 18, 84
Export Processing Zones, 55, 83
Externalization, 5, 22, 29, 74

F
Fanon, Frantz, 72
Filipino community, 11
Financial elites, 62
Foreign direct investment, 28
French colonialism, 72
Fundamental rights, vii, 24

G
Gated communities, 10, 62
Gentrification, 2, 11, 61, 76, 78, 79

Giddens, Anthony, 30n2
Glick Schiller, Nina, viii, 19, 20, 43
Globality, 19
Globalization, 19, 40, 41, 44, 45
Global political economy, and migration systems, 54–60
Goldin, Ian, 64n2
Goodin, Robert, 30n5, 81, 82, 86n3
Groupism, 30n3

H
Hall, Stuart, 84
Harvey, David, 56, 83
Hierarchy, 5, 17, 63, 80, 81, 84, 85, 93
Higgin, Peter, 26, 30n5
Hobbes, Thomas, 18, 23
Hollifield, James, ixn3
Hukou system, 62
Human mobility, 21

I
Identification documents, 38
Illegalized immigrants, 8
Imbroscio, David L., 64n4
IMF, 28
Immigrants, 8, 19, 72, 75
  deskilling\brain waste, 61
  detention, 31n16
Immigration, 25, 27, 29n1
  enforcement, 31n16
  issue, 93
  offices, 22
  policy, 75
International border regimes, 6
International migrants, 2, 20, 26, 62, 63, 74, 78
International non-governmental organizations (INGOs), 43
Italian migrants, 39

J
Jacobson, Matthew Frye, 57

K
Kassovitz, 70, 71
Keynes, John Maynard, 92
King, Natasha, 77
King, Russell, 43, 74
Kukathas, Chandran, 62

L
Labor markets, 55
L'affaire du foulard, 73
La Haine, 12, 69–75, 85, 86
  police brutality, 70–74
The Law of Peoples, 18
Lefebrve, Henri, 71
Leviathan, 18
Libya, 23, 73, 85
Low-wage jobs, 62
Low-wage workers, 10, 55

M
Madanipour, Ali, 75
Martins, Hermínio, 18
Mazzadra, Sandro, 9, 46
M'Bowolé, Makom, 70
Methodological nationalism, vii–viii, 3, 4, 6, 7, 10–12, 12n1, 18–20, 22–25, 27–29, 30n2, 37, 38, 40–42, 45, 48, 53, 59–61, 64, 69, 74, 79, 80, 92, 95
Methodological statism, 13n1
Migrants, 2, 26
  Illegalized, 7, 28, 62, 75, 77 (*see also unauthorized migrants*)
  labor, 55
  strangers, outsiders, 94

Migrants (*cont.*)
  unauthorized, 5–7, 22, 29 (*see also* *illegalized migrants*)
  undocumented, *see* migrants, unauthorized
Migration, vii, 5, 19
  controls, 45
  internal, 2, 4, 5, 20, 21, 27, 54, 55, 61, 63, 79, 93
  international, 55
  justice, 7
  political philosophy of, 23–29
Migration systems
  distributive justice, 58
  and global political economy, 54
Mill, Charles W., 30n4
Miller, David, 6, 9, 26, 30n5
Mobility, 2, 42
  barriers in, 3
  restrictions within states, 60
  turn, 7, 42, 93
Moch, Leslie Page, 1, 2
Moses, Jonathan, 62
Muslim ban, 93
Muslims, 72
  appearance of, 73

N
Nail, Thomas, 5, 9, 30n10, 39, 62, 81
Nation building, viii, 18–20, 22, 38, 43, 84, 85, 95
Nation-state, vii–viii, 3, 4, 7, 9, 10, 12, 18–23, 25, 30n3, 37–49, 53, 54, 56, 58, 59, 61, 79, 82–84, 86, 93, 94
  definition of, 59
Native-born citizens, 8, 31n15
Neilson, Brett, 9, 46, 47
NGO workers, 92
No Borders scholarship, 76
Nomadism, 6

Nomadology, 39
Non-discrimination, 27
Nozickian libertarianism, 24

O
Open borders, 10, 24, 25, 76, 77, 79
Opportunity hoarding, 63, 84
Organizational migrants, 26

P
Parreñas, Rhacel Salazar, 11
Pateman, Carole, 30n4
Pitts, Jennifer, 85
Political
  exclusion, 84
  philosophy, ixn2, 17
  theory, ixn2
  transnationalism, 44
Political Liberalism, 18
Pritchett, Lant, 83
Push/pull explanations, 21, 56

R
The Racial Contract, 30n4
Rawlsian egalitarianism, 24
Rawls, John, 18, 23, 29n1, 85
Refugees, 46, 58, 73, 75, 76, 85
  fleeing persecution, 93
Right to City, 71
Rumford, Chris, 8, 9, 44–47
Rural populations, 61
Rushdie, Salman, ixn4

S
Sager, Alex, 30n9, 31n16, 64n1, 86n3
Salazar Parreñas, Rhacel, 11
Sassen, Saskia, 28, 40, 55
Schiller, Nina Glick, viii, 19

Scott, James C., 6, 40
Secure visas, 57
Sedentarian bias, 3–5
Sedentarism, 4–7, 41
Seglow, Jonathan, 26, 30n5, 82
Segregation, 10, 11, 54, 59, 61, 63, 76, 78, 79, 93
Semi-citizenship, 63
Sen, Amartya, 80, 82, 86n7, 94
The Sexual Contract, 30n4
Smith, Anthony, 12n1, 19, 30n12
Social contract theory, 23, 30n4
Social scientific cosmopolitanism, 80
South-North migration, 26
South-South migration, 26
Sovereignty, 5, 20, 23, 27, 28, 42, 77
State borders, 5, 11, 21, 22, 25, 46, 48, 59, 61, 76, 79, 86n4
State-centrism, 30n3
State monopolization, 38
State sovereignty, methodological nationalism, 20–21

T
Temporary migration, 26
Territorialism, 30n3
Territorial trap, 45
Terrorism, 40, 75
Theory of Justice, 18
Tiber River, 11
Tilly, Charles, 84
Tourism, 2, 20
Trade agreements, 28
Transit migration, 26

Transmigrants, 43
Transnationalism, viii, 7–9, 29, 41–48, 53, 79, 80
Transnational migration, 43, 45

U
Unauthorized migrants, 7
Utilitarianism, 24
Utopianism, 76

V
Vallet, Élisabeth, 45
Valls, Andrew, 86n5
Visa-free travel, 42
Visas
  secure, 57
  work, 7

W
Wacquant, Loïc, 72, 74
Walzer, Michael, vii, 30n6, 86n4
Wellman, Christopher Heath, 26, 30n5
Wimmer, Andreas, viii, 19, 20
Work visas, 7
World Economic Forum, 43
World Social Forum, 43
The Wretched of the Earth, 72

Y
Young, Iris Marion, 64n4

CPSIA information can be obtained
at www.ICGtesting.com
Printed in the USA
LVHW081144120519
617530LV00030B/2284/P